MAGNETIC
MARKETING

MAGNETIC
MARKETING

HOW TO ATTRACT A FLOOD OF NEW CUSTOMERS THAT **PAY, STAY,** AND **REFER**

DAN S. KENNEDY

WITH THE **MAGNETIC MARKETING** TEAM

ForbesBooks

Published by ForbesBooks, Charleston, South Carolina.
Member of Advantage Media Group.

ForbesBooks is a registered trademark, and the ForbesBooks colophon is a trademark of Forbes Media, LLC.

Printed in the United States of America.

10 9 8 7 6 5 4 3 2 1

Advantage Media Group is proud to be a part of the Tree Neutral® program. Tree Neutral offsets the number of trees consumed in the production and printing of this book by taking proactive steps such as planting trees in direct proportion to the number of trees used to print books. To learn more about Tree Neutral, please visit **www.treeneutral.com.**

Since 1917, the Forbes mission has remained constant. Global Champions of Entrepreneurial Capitalism. ForbesBooks exists to further that aim by bringing the Stories, Passion, and Knowledge of top thought leaders to the forefront. ForbesBooks brings you The Best in Business. To be considered for publication, please visit **www.forbesbooks.com.**

Never Again Be An Advertising Victim, Discover The Secrets To Creating A <u>Successful Advertising and Marketing System For Your Business, Products and Services...</u>

Get _THE_ System That Business Owners Just Like You Have Used To Radically Transform Their Advertising From Ineffective and Wasteful Into A Business Asset That Will <u>Predictably and Reliably Deliver A Steady Stream Of New Customers, Clients, Patients and</u>

Profits to the Bottom Line!

In This Master Class, You'll Discover:

- The difference between **Lead Generation** and **Brand Building**, and why lead generation almost always **TRUMPS** the latter.

- In most cases, THIS one form of advertising is only **wasting your time and money** for **minimal results.**

- THIS form of advertising will have you **seeing returns in days, weeks, or months** instead of wondering what the expense brought to you in return a year down the road.

- How YOU can be successful **without having to worry about how many people know your brand by name.**

- Learn how advertising in certain media outlets that have **nothing** to do with your business can actually make **A LOT** of sense and be **very beneficial.**

- How to **model** the marketing strategies of national companies in a way that will their success into a local level.

Table of Contents

BUILDING YOUR MAGNETIC MARKETING SYSTEM

Learn the Secrets of the Most Successful Business Owners Who Have Created a Flood of New Customers, Clients, or Patients

You have finally found it!

The one place created for entrepreneurs and business owners BY entrepreneurs and business owners seeking to finally answer that common, nagging question:

"Why am I working harder and not seeing more money?"

All business owners, regardless of their current success or lack of success, are stuck—either you are growing or you're dying. There is no middle ground. Which leaves you with great opportunity.

You have worked hard, created a good business with a steady revenue, a somewhat reliable customer base, and profit margins that at least keep you above water.

Yet, you feel like the proverbial hamster on the wheel. You keep running faster and faster and yet you can't seem to break that cycle. Every day feels like a struggle just to keep your head above water. You're wondering what happened to that dream of owning a business—a dream where you didn't have to worry about money, where you could take an afternoon off care free to watch your child's school play. What happened to that dream?

You've tried marketing: you've spent serious money on ads that didn't work, direct mail that under-delivered, Pay-Per-Click advertising that has drained your bank account dry, and probably a host of other approaches, none of which have delivered the results promised or expected.

Like most business owners, you sometimes feel confused and overwhelmed; getting hammered on all sides with "advisors" saying do one thing or another after another; and feeling like you have to press harder, to do more and more—just to get the same results. Or less.

I'm here to help you—to mute all that noise and provide you with a set of principles (not tactics) and the resources to magnetically attract clients who are ready, willing and able to move forward with you.

And by resources, I mean my duplicatable machine for not only attracting clients, but converting clients and multiplying one client into two.

Marketing is an ever-changing world, as new media seems to pop up every day, but if you learn the principles that allow you to magnetically attract clients, you can make any media at any time work. When you develop a system that feeds you new clients on a daily basis, you will never feel the anxiety of wondering when or where your next client will come from! In fact, you can finally take a vacation without checking your phone every hour.

If you're at least open to the notion that maybe, just maybe there's a better way forward than the one you've traveled thus far—and if you're reading this now with an open mind willing to cautiously believe in that possibility...

Then this book is for you.

WHY I WROTE THIS BOOK

I'm here to offer a radical and challenging idea that just about everything you think you know and have been conditioned to believe about growing your business is wrong.

I am here to mute the noise and guide you to clarity about a relatively short list of fundamental principles and strategies that can prevent you from being lost in a dense forest of media demanding your attention, time, and money.

If you get it, you'll smack yourself in the head for not seeing it all sooner, on your own. You'll be in awe of how much sense it makes. You'll never look at an ad, sales letter or website the same again. Traditional advertising and marketing will be ruined for you.

But let me warn you—when you do get it, you'll also be criticized by employees, argued with by everyone, and ridiculed by even family and friends. You will need your results and a steel spine to stay strong. The outstanding results you'll see when shifting from ordinary marketing to response-driven marketing will convince you. You will need courage and discipline to stay your new course.

I promise you that being thought a "fool" or "misguided renegade" and having millions of dollars trumps being thought of as "normal" and "correct" and "proper" and barely making a living.

WHERE DID THESE IDEAS ORIGINATE?

These ideas began with a discovery—or more accurately, a series of discoveries—that could well form the most important realization you will ever arrive at as a business person. It's disappointing and frustrating at first, but empowering if embraced and acted upon.

I discovered:

➜ You can have the most wonderful product or greatest service ever invented and still starve.

➜ You can be a spectacular sales person and still starve.

➜ You can have a positive attitude that Norman Vincent Peale would envy and be as motivated as a participant at a Tony Robbins seminar and still starve.

➜ You can be a master closer, closing sales at will left and right, and still starve.

➜ You can provide great value, great service, and great expertise and still starve.

➜ Your business can literally be a paragon of virtues, with the world seemingly singing your praises 24/7, and even as you bask in their applause, you can still starve.

The realization you must come to is this: you could very well starve, you won't get rich, and you certainly won't have peace of mind...

Unless and until you have an affordable, efficient, dependable means of attracting a sufficient flow of qualified LEADS and BUYERS.

Most business owners sort of know this but they still focus on everything but the one thing that will make all the difference in the world to their success: **Marketing.**

All the frustrations and internal problems you're experiencing with your business today are because you DON'T have a good Marketing System.

Many businesses have good products, good services—all that and more—but they fail because they can't give themselves enough sales opportunities. To paraphrase Thoreau, most business owners lead lives of desperation because they don't know how to create a steady and sufficient supply of qualified customers.

IT'S TIME FOR A DIFFERENT VISION

I've been teaching these principles in various forms since the mid-1970s—due to the dire economic conditions at that time, I referred to them as "The Small Business Emergency Survival Kit." They have gradually grown into the system I call "*Magnetic Marketing*" today, which has quickly spread throughout the United States and all over the world.

The principles in this book have been tested over and over again, not just by myself, but by entrepreneurs and business owners of all shapes, sizes, locations, and industries. Today, we have students in 167 different countries using these principles to create a steady flow of new customers, clients, or patients in their businesses. They use these strategies to scale, grow, and differentiate their businesses—to rise above price competition and to quickly demand (and receive) top dollar for their services.

As you read through this book, you may feel as if you have heard pieces of this before. I hope you have. I have been sharing these principles since the 1970's. Hundreds of thousands heard my message when I was on the SUCCESS Tour, have purchased my training programs, have participated in my coaching groups, or have been private clients. Thanks to Magnetic Marketing, this message, these principles and their influence continue to grow. There are many out there teaching these ideas, some give me credit, some don't.

Today, you are hearing the entire story, straight from the horse's mouth.

Today, I am here to give you the entire vision plus the architecture that will allow you to make this vision a reality.

The vision of being the prosperous owner of a real business— not of random or episodic income events, not of endless need for the next new promotion, not of frequent worry where the next sale might come from.

The vision of certainty and security and stability. Of a continuous and steady inflow of desired customers, clients, patients, subscribers, or members. Even of creating equity and wealth, not just day to day income.

The vision based on two specific promises I'll make concerning what you'll discover as you go through this book:

1. I promise to take you beyond just another trick or two that might increase conversion on a website temporarily or that everybody is excited about momentarily and instead, show you a SYSTEM for marketing that you can quickly begin using to make significantly more money across ALL your communication channels and media choices.

2. I will—in this book—reveal the powerful, proven secrets to attracting opportunity, customers and clients in abundance, and creating sustainable businesses. You'll realize what you must build for yourself to create true freedom, stability, and scalability in your business.

You do NOT need any special background, education, or skills to use this—other than commitment to use it. You can apply it to any kind of business serving any kind of market. I have students using what I'll share here with businesses in health, retail, fitness, finance, coaching, trades—you name it. You'll meet people later who'll demonstrate exactly how this SYSTEM worked for them.

For now, know that YOU CAN turbo-charge your ability to magnetically attract and achieve with what you'll discover on the following pages.

Let's begin.

P.S. You do NOT need to read this entire book before also taking some next steps to connect with me and with Magnetic Marketing. Feel free to take advantage of the invitations on the next page NOW.

FOUNDATIONS OF MAGNETIC MARKETING

CHAPTER 1

What If Everything You've Ever Been Told About Growing a Business Was Wrong?

I am sorry to tell you that you have been lied to for a very long time!

Note that I didn't use softer words like "misled," "mis-informed," "offered less than optimal advice." Nope. I laid it out straight and plain.

You've been **lied to**.

It's critical to your success that I open your eyes to this fact. And I hope you're interested in the blunt, unvarnished truth about what entrepreneurs and business owners actually do to create top income, wealth, independence, and sustainability. Frankly, not everyone is ready for such a conversation. Many prefer excuses to achievement. Others prefer fantasy to reality.

What I'm about to teach you will radically alter how you acquire customers, clients or patients, and boost your sales and profits. I have a track record of forty-five-plus years creating multi-millionaires and seven-figure income earners. I am a made-from-scratch multi-millionaire, serial entrepreneur and I'm doing real work in the trenches right now, working with real clients and solving real issues. In fact, in one recent year alone, the combined revenues of my small cadre of private clients exceeded $1 billion.

And every marketing plan I've ever devised for any client—and they now number in the hundreds and hundreds, commanding fees exceeding $100,000 plus royalties—has been based on the SYSTEM I'm going to reveal in this book.

This book is for entrepreneurs, business owners, professional services practices, coaches and consultants. It pulls back the curtain on real world strategies I've revealed to the thousands of entrepreneurs just like you who have subscribed to my **No B.S. Marketing Letter**, and use my systems to transform "ordinary" businesses into extraordinary money machines that far outperform their industry norms, peers, competitors and the wildest imagination of the owners.

How do they do it?

By making the strategic switch from traditional advertising to a response-driven advertising strategy we call "**Magnetic Marketing**."

Magnetic Marketing was created to help entrepreneurs and business owners—with NO marketing knowledge or expertise—and empower them to create compelling marketing on their own without hiring outside help.

Magnetic Marketing has impacted thousands of businesses, professions, industries, product and service categories, literally changing the way their customers are obtained. (Indeed, today they form what could well be called a "secret society" of people who have figured it out.)

Its roots go back decades, if not centuries. Its core foundational principle is that every advertisement, promotion, email, flyer, TV commercial, etc. focuses ALL energy on:

→ **identifying exactly who you want to be your customer, client, or patient, and**

→ **getting them to respond in a specific way—not wasting any effort on branding, image, humor, style or anything else.**

THIS is the kind of marketing we'll discuss in this book—marketing designed to "magnetically attract" in a specific, repeatable, measurable way. And this is the ONLY model of marketing that you as a entrepreneur and business owner should model and use.

When you embrace this, you become part of a movement that I started over two decades ago and that's now carried on by the company I founded thirty-eight years ago, **Magnetic Marketing**, which continues to provide powerful marketing and business growth strategies to maximize the success of entrepreneurs and business owners all over the world—a rare feat considering how many companies have come and gone over that period of time.

LET'S DISPEL THE MYTHS...

Personally, early on I went through a painful phase of thinking where I believed that I should be successful by my willingness to work hard and by offering products and services that were truly valuable.

As logical as this may sound, it's merely a painful myth. I still struggled.

And so I immersed myself in self-help, personal improvement, and motivational materials. I said affirmations. I thought only positive thoughts. I believed. And still I struggled—even with great products and what I believed was a great mindset to go with them.

My life only changed when it dawned on me that great was no better than lousy if I had no able, willing, ready buyers to present great to.

This is the key realization.

Without a sufficient and steady stream of people with whom you can exchange value for money, nothing else about your business matters. Not your most excellent website. Not your high visibility location. Not your credentials, degrees, certifications, education, etc.

Not your hard-working "nose-to-the-grindstone" ethic.

Being more talented or skilled than others in your area of expertise has ZERO value if you cannot harness the principles and power of *magnetic attraction* in a practical way.

Having the very best, most innovative, most beneficial products or services has ZERO value if you cannot harness the principles and power of *magnetic attraction* in a practical way.

Many harm themselves by denying or decrying this reality. They desperately want to believe that better is better... having better credentials... having gone to a better school... having more and better experience... having more and better integrity... better work ethic, better at paying your dues... etc. BETTER *SHOULD* BE ENOUGH.

Maybe in an idyllic and just world that would be so.

But not in THIS world.

In this world, you are not automatically awarded what you deserve or think you deserve. It's not a pure meritocracy. If that were the case, there'd probably be no rich porn stars and no poor pastors and preachers. I have learned and taught that money moves about for its own reasons, and neither need nor deservingness are magnetic to it.

It depends on powerful, well-crafted, measurable strategies— a tried and true system—rooted in common sense and that works across all kinds of media. The strategies that we'll talk about have been applied in 136 different business categories, by over 93,417 entrepreneurs in 167 different countries—they deliver.

In other words, *Magnetic Marketing* is as proven as the law of gravity. I tell you this because it may require some patience from you for you to really get it and use it, but like gravity, you cannot defy its facts.

This switch is critical because…

YOU'VE BEEN SET UP TO FAIL

If you've managed to survive even a year or two in business, it's obvious that you've gone well beyond the limited framework provided by our "educational system" when it comes to grasping the core principles of marketing.

But even with the scant marketing education business owners may have acquired from school, mentors, and self-schooling, the fact is that most of them are like the blind leading the blind. Even the highly vaunted MBA accreditations typically fail to deliver serious "real-world," bottom-line results when put to the test of facing the dog-eat-dog frenzy of the marketplace.

I set before you as proof—and is a law much like gravity is, you can not fix it, you can only know it and change your actions to fit into the section you want to. The financial reality is that in every profession, every category of business, every sales team, every population, these figures hold true:

→ 1% create tremendous incomes and wealth

→ 4% do very well

→ 15% earn good livings

→ 60% struggle endlessly

→ 20% fail

In a nutshell, 80 percent do poorly / 20 percent succeed.

Why then would you want to copy the marketing done by the majority when facts show it FAILS THEM? Why should you follow that same path to frustration and failure?

Most "ordinary" businesses believe they have to advertise and market like much bigger brand-name companies, so they invest (waste) lots of money in many different kinds of media to promote image, brand, and presence.

You CANNOT make the mistake of jumping into media because "everyone else is using it." Big name brands have all sorts of reasons for the way they advertise and market that have ZERO to do with getting a customer or making sales. Your agenda is much simpler—in fact, there's a huge difference between how BIG corporations consider marketing and how you as a entrepreneur and business owner sees it.

Big Corporation Agenda for Advertising and Marketing

→ Please/appease its board of directors (most of whom know zip about advertising and marketing but have lots of opinions).
→ Please/appease its stockholders.
→ Look good and appropriate to Wall Street.
→ Look good and appropriate to the media.
→ Build brand identity.
→ Win awards for advertising.
→ Sell something.

YOUR Agenda

→ Sell something. NOW!

I realized a long time ago that big dumb corporations were using sloppy, wasteful "mass advertising" practices that had them hemorrhaging money left and right.

But that didn't stop entrepreneurs and businesses owners from "modeling" what they saw-read-heard every day, wrongly thinking that "if it works for them, it's gotta work for us too."

> **Here's the No B.S. Truth:** The typical entrepreneur and business owner is essentially clueless when it comes to advertising and marketing. This makes them highly vulnerable to becoming what I call "Advertising Victims"—easy prey for media salespeople, ad agencies, and anyone else who doesn't know how to actually close the deal and make a sale.

Think I'm wrong?

If you ever manage to corner a business owner, try to get him to tell you with confidence WHERE his customers and sales come from, what it costs to get a customer, what kind of results does one ad get versus another. Try. He can't. He's guessing. And that's what the industry vultures rely on, they know that when their customer (i.e., YOU) can only guess how well their marketing works, they have a credit card they can ding regularly and without fail.

I realized something different had to be done, because entrepreneurs and business owners need a saner, more productive path to business growth that makes their business life more pleasant, lucrative, and certain.

AND IT'S NOT ABOUT WORKING HARDER

You've been told over and over again that the answer to all your troubles is to:

→ Work Harder

→ Work Smarter

→ Work Harder and Smarter

Sorry, but none of those will fly or even come close to hitting the mark.

It's not about working harder and being smarter about how you do so. I'm willing to wager you've already gone down that road and have done all you can do and the results just weren't there.

You don't need more hard work... not from yourself, your spouse, your staff—nobody. Instead, you need a NEW strategy. You need a SYSTEM—one that works for you, 24/7/365 doing all this for you:

→ A system that generates a predictable flow of new customers, clients, and patients

→ A system that turns every customer into two customers

→ A system that creates repeatable business

→ A system that allows you freedom (financial and time)

→ A system focused on marketing

The more productive answer is to develop a SYSTEM that attracts new customers, clients, or patients to you in an organized way.

WHY NOW IS THE RIGHT TIME
FOR THIS NEW SYSTEM

The system I'm about to reveal to you in this book will radically change your thinking about what you invest your time in, what's truly important when it comes to making money, and the way you communicate your ideas, products, services and worth to the world.

It's a much more sophisticated way of creating power for yourself in a cluttered marketplace. *A systematic way to magnetically attract your ideal customers, clients, or patients.*

A system that gives you reliable and predictable results so you finally know when you invest X dollars, you can expect Y number of leads, then Z number of appointments or selling opportunities.

You want a system that enables you to better target the most appropriate and valuable customers for your business, so you're not wasting time, energy, resources scurrying down rabbit holes chasing "would-be" customers who in fact will "never-be."

Most importantly, you need a system you can comprehend and control.

It's just too complicated to wing it on your own anymore. Way back when, I managed my own mailings with a printout of the prospect list, a stack of envelopes, and an occasionally amenable cat to lick the stamps. It worked great for me then, but today's barrage of media options makes such a simple operation not only outdated, but terribly self-limiting. Media choices abound and multi-channel marketing funnels that best leverage the unique strengths of each is the proper path. You can't succeed with a haphazard approach.

You MUST follow a well-conceived, testable, scalable, practical system—and you've come to the right person to reveal just such a system to you.

THEY CALL ME "THE PROFESSOR OF HARSH REALITY"

It's a title I proudly embrace. Reality and life have always been harsh. As Hollywood legend John Wayne once said:

"Life is hard. And it's harder if you're stupid."

In forty-five years of helping all kinds of entrepreneurs and businesses achieve their dreams, I've realized that business owners aren't actually "stupid" when it comes to raw cerebral horsepower. The problem lies in the "stupid" things they do that they've been led to believe are true.

That may seem a bit blunt, or even a bit uncomfortable. Good.

I unapologetically wrote this book to offer the **blunt, unvarnished truth** about how entrepreneurs and business owners really CAN create a flood of new customers, clients, and patients while building wealth, independence and sustainability.

There are a lot of numbers bandied about in marketing—response percentages, circulation, pass-along effect, visitors, dedicated visitors, likes, friends, fans, and on and on. I'm here to tell you it's all B.S. It's all about leads that convert to income. Period.

And the very worst number in business is ONE. If you are over-dependent on any ONE thing in your business, you will—at some point—be punished for this vulnerability. You can bank on that. One key person, one key account or client, one product, one service, one skill, one technology—all woefully insecure and unstable. This is particularly true of MEDIA.

It's about attracting more customers who respect and value what you do so much so that they are willing to pay for it. It's not about just bringing in more (quantity), it's about bringing in more of the right people (quality).

And the foundational key to making this happen…

YOU MUST SEPARATE YOURSELF FROM THE COMPETITION

I want you to understand, whatever your deliverables are, they are not your business.

You must make yourself the go-to person, place, or entity for some audience that can be interested in you and your deliverables. And the primary way to accomplish this is by crafting an answer to this question:

"Why should I choose you versus any and every other provider of the same product or service that you provide?"

Resolved with what legendary ad man Rosser Reeves called a *USP*, a *Unique Selling Proposition*.

Tremendous turnarounds in business have taken place as the result of great USPs. Domino's Pizza was originally driven by a marketing message which everybody came to know, *"Fresh hot pizza delivered in thirty minutes or less, guaranteed."*

If you dissect it, you'll see some interesting things. First of all, it doesn't claim to be all things to all people. There's no mention of mama's recipe from the old country. No mention of a special sauce. In fact, there's not even any mention of *good* pizza. All it says is that it is going to get to you while it's still hot and it's still fresh and that they guarantee to do that.

What is your USP? This is going to take a little bit of work. Somewhere in your business, there is a good answer. If not, you need to make one.

Unfortunately, the first thing one does when we start to talk about Unique Selling Proposition is to jump to the conclusion that there is nothing special about their business. Sometimes in rare instances, that's true. That's when you have to do some creative thinking about your business to make it into something unique.

Here are three questions you can ask yourself to help kick-start the process of finding or creating your USP.

1. What specifically do you do that's truly different compared to competitors?

For Domino's, it was originally being there in thirty minutes or less. More recently, they revolutionized the company against badly sagging sales by taking the worst ranked pizza to the best ranked for taste and quality. But that's actually the ante to already being in the game.

2. How do you uniquely benefit your target market?

J.K. Rowling of the *Harry Potter* books and her publisher made each new book's release of exceptional benefit to independent bookstores with a devised plan for big events, books held back to release at midnight, drawing huge numbers of kids and parents into these stores milling about at a party, in costume, snacking and browsing and buying other books for an hour or more before the clock struck midnight.

The target market, the bookstore owner, was uniquely benefited in reciprocity. Rowling got far more promotional work out of the store owners than hundreds of other authors of other children's fantasy books.

3. <u>Can you niche your target market in a way nobody else can or will?</u>

One of my students, a lawyer named Bill Hammond, created Alzheimer's Law, a subset of elder law essentially wrapping traditional estate planning, Medicare and Medicaid planning, and other family legal matters inside a differently described package, positioned for families with a senior showing signs of or having been diagnosed with dementia. This enabled Bill to use the exact lead generation strategies laid out in this system.

Take the time to create your own USP—it's one of the greatest marketing weapons you can ever have for your product(s) or your business.

CHAPTER 2

Why Marketing Fails

Over the course of this book, you're going to discover a totally new and different way to market your products and services.

In fact, you could consider this "an alternative universe" of marketing, where all the fundamentals you thought were true have been turned on their head. Kind of like that episode in Star Trek where Captain Kirk was a bad guy and Spock sported an eminently logical goatee.

It's important that you set aside any preconceptions you might have about changing gears with your marketing, because the fact of the matter is clear and has been for years. Indeed, way back in 2006, long before the explosion of social media like Facebook, LinkedIn, Instagram, YouTube, and much more, I wrote something that remains as true today as ever:

Most small business advertising and marketing STINKS.

I stand by this still. Monstrous sums are wasted and opportunities lost. Even amid all the change in technology and practically limitless options available to get your message out, nothing has changed for the better. In fact, if anything, it's gotten worse.

Businesspeople are really confused and overwhelmed—told they must do this, that, the other thing, more and more—just to get the same results.

I'm here to guide you to clarity about a relatively short list of mistakes that, when understood and addressed, can safeguard your sanity from the assault of a thousand points of media options demanding your attention, time, and money.

MISTAKE #1: MARKETING TO THE WRONG PEOPLE

Most businesses market to the wrong people. When their marketing fails to deliver, they blame it on something else, as in it's not pretty enough, it's not big enough, we didn't get the messaging right, the billboard's stuck in the wrong location, we didn't advertise in the right magazine or on the right cable channel or whatever.

I'm not saying that any of these factors AREN'T a problem. They very well could play a role in any ad's success or lack thereof.

But the **bigger problem** is the simple fact that in most cases, most advertising is not directed at any one person. Instead, it's directed at EVERYONE.

The marketing lacks a clear understanding of WHO they are trying to target.

And here's the rub. Unless you have extremely deep pockets like one of the giant multinational corporations, you CAN'T market to everyone. You have to discriminate. It's not a bad word, in fact it's your safe passage to focus and prosperity.

When you focus on a specific WHO, you're able to hone in on exactly what makes that person tick. You're able to adjust your offers and your messaging in a way that perfectly matches their desires and abilities to fulfill those desires. Knowing that WHO inside and out enables you to craft a compelling, emotional message that reaches deep into their hopes, dreams, fears, and pain.

At any given moment in time, only 5 percent at best, are intellectually, emotionally, practically and financially ready to act on or make a buying decision about your product, service or proposition. Inevitably, 95 percent of most advertising falls on "deaf ears." This makes it imperative to "hit the bullseye" with the 5 percent, by narrowing your focus. However, you can and should also scheme to get those who aren't ready but will be to raise their hands early, and we'll get to this later in this book.

MISTAKE #2: SAYING THE WRONG THINGS

Not only does your marketing have to talk to the right person, it has to say the right things to that person. When you say something that fails to connect with your target customer, we call that a failed "Message to Market Match."

Going back to my example of Domino's USP, they understood their initial market perfectly—ravenously hungry college students desperate for something, anything, to ease the munchies. Their message was "fresh hot pizza in thirty minutes or less, guaranteed"— the perfect solution delivered to your doorstep in record time. THAT is a perfect "Message to Market Match."

What makes it even more powerful is that they entered the conversation going on inside their customer's head—which in simple terms could be boiled down to "Hungry. Food. Now."

Had they instead focused on "delicious sauce, mama's old country recipe, ingredients sourced from the finest, all organic farms, delivered in style by a man in a tuxedo…" it would have tanked. Because that's NOT what the market was looking for and it certainly didn't match the dialogue taking place in that college kid's mind as he was watching the TV or studying for finals.

Another key mistake many make involves the language used in the marketing. When you focus on a specific group of people, you're able to tap into the vocabulary they use every day. Doing so is critical—for example, with musicians (and magicians) you would want to promise them "more gigs" not "more jobs." Golfers have a vernacular all their own as well, with "bunkers," "buried lies," "shanks," and "skulled shots a.k.a. wormburners." Just like you wouldn't attempt to communicate with a Frenchman in Mandarin Chinese, you don't want to use "outsider" language and terminology when communicating a sales message to your prospective customer.

To our 1970s pizza-eating college student now approaching seasoned citizen status, it's not about hearing a little better—that's not worth spending the money on. He can crank up sound system and The Rolling Stones will sound as good as ever. The real problem, which IS worth investing in, is not hearing what my kids are saying, them thinking I'm losing my mind because I'm not responding, and them then sending me off to the old folks' home because of that.

You only know this when you truly know your WHO. You need to know more than just their demographics, you need to know their hopes, dreams, fears, and most importantly, the conversations that are going on in their heads—the things they will never tell you.

MISTAKE #3: ASKING THEM TO DO THE WRONG THINGS

This boils down to asking for the sale too quickly without first narrowing down our universe of potential buyers.

We live in an extremely skeptical age. Once-respected professions and institutions now have practically zero credibility, including journalists, clergy, education providers, and so many more. And even lower than politicians rank the oily, slimy salesman who's all-too-eager to shake your hand and pluck your purse.

Making a sale—especially for something that's largely intangible as a service—requires asking a person to take a leap of faith. Without first establishing a significant level of trust in your credibility, responsibility, and authority right from the get-go, you face a significant uphill battle enticing anyone to do anything, let alone sign on the dotted line.

Therefore, instead of going right for the sale out the gate to everyone on the planet, a more effective marketing strategy is to first narrow down your focus by getting a subset of your potential market to qualify themselves by "raising their hand" in response to an offer that's much easier to say "yes" to—a free gift of some sort, possibly a video or a report. This enables you to begin that process of gathering a group of people who have a problem you can solve. It enables you to begin establishing credibility, authority, and trust, turning an unknown, potential customer into a self-acknowledged "lead" with whom you can follow up more intensely and personally.

We call this concept "lead generation" and we'll discuss it in much greater detail in just a bit.

MISTAKE #4: THINKING YOU CAN ADVERTISE ANYWHERE AND EVERYWHERE

Marketing used to be relatively simple when it came to choosing which media platform to use. CBS. NBC. ABC. PBS. Local radio. Local newspapers. Yellow Pages. A limited number of high profile magazines. Billboards. And the few other outlying options of varying effectiveness, such as skywriting, smoke signals, and a strange new technology that was called "the world wide web."

As the giant reptiles vanished from our planet, so too has disappeared this once-simple media menu. Today, you as a marketer face a far more complicated, diverse, and challenging array of options from which to choose. New media channels and technologies seem to appear daily.

This constantly changing media landscape challenges even the most tech-savvy marketer. Not only do you have to keep up with the latest and greatest, you face disruptions caused by shifting public opinion, government intervention, and even changes to corporate strategy. Google adjusts its search algorithms continuously, potentially rendering an easily found, SEO-optimized website practically invisible. In regards to Pay-Per Click (PPC) ads, whole businesses were destroyed when the infamous "Google Slap" completely shut down lead generation ads and systems that previously delivered handsome returns.

Because of this overwhelming complexity, many business owners simply throw up their hands and hand this task over to a so-called expert or ad salesman and then write the checks based on them saying "you have to be on xxxx."

The only way to avoid this mistake is to nail down exactly the WHO to whom you are selling. Once you know that, it's actually quite simple to choose which media channels to advertise in—you go where they go.

If they're on Facebook, you go on Facebook. If they read *Model Railroading*, you advertise in *Model Railroading* (and note—what you sell inside *Model Railroading* doesn't even have to relate in the slightest to trains, it just needs to appeal to the kind of person who reads that magazine).

And even though many consider them outdated, the Yellow Pages can still offer huge benefits to marketers if they're targeting an older demographic who relies on their use.

You want to only be where your who is and then you want to EVERYWHERE they are.

It's a huge mistake to try to sort out all the different options for media without first having a plan for what you intend to use that media for. The worst thing you can do is a series of random, disconnected marketing attempts across various media channels. Instead, you want to create a true system that attracts new customers in an organized way. Because it's only with this kind of system that you can achieve reliable, predictable results—so you know when you invest X you will get Y in return.

MISTAKE #5: NO MARKETING SYSTEM

This is probably one of the biggest, most widespread mistakes made: Marketing without a system.

Without a system, you are flying blind, literally throwing jello against a wall, seeing if any of it sticks, and if, by happenstance, something does work, you have no way of leveraging that data because anything that did produce a positive result is now an oozing green puddle on the office floor.

Without a system you're forced to pray for and then rely on one-hit wonders (e.g., remember the "Macarena"?) which offer you a brief moment in the sunshine of success, but then vanish like dust in the wind. It worked, but you don't know why, you can't repeat the process, and once it's gone, it's gone.

This goes hand in hand with what I call "Rollercoaster Marketing"—where, when times get tough and customers are scarce, you throw everything plus the kitchen sink into your marketing efforts. If you're lucky and manage to catch a bit of traction, your funnel gets filled up and your business starts the ascent. So you drop everything and get to work, because you're now too busy to market and the inevitable perception is that you don't need to because everything's fat and happy. But this only delays the inevitable, because when you stop marketing, your funnel will eventually dry up—new customers stop coming in, existing clients move on—so you start the descent, howling all the way to the bottom. And you're back to where you started.

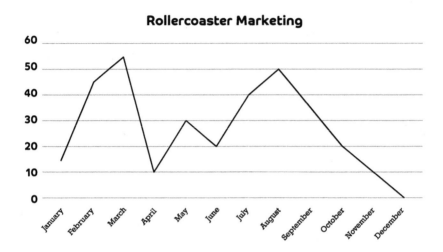

Having a reliable, scientific, and predictable marketing system is what you must put in place instead. You want a system where marketing works like a faucet that you can turn on or off depending on the needs of your business and where you want to go with it.

At a minimum, you want your Marketing System to focus on three key areas:

1. Lead generation—the ongoing acquisition of leads for your business

2. Conversion—taking those leads and converting them into paying customers

3. Retention/Referral—keeping that customer-base intact and generating new leads based on referrals.

Once you have this system set up, you simply put it in motion and let 'er run. I have clients who have Magnetic Marketing Systems that have been running untouched for seven to ten years.

MISTAKE #6: CHASING CLIENTS

Almost as big a mistake as not having a system is the wrong-headed perception by business owners of all stripes that it's your job to CHASE customers, clients, or patients. While it may seem logical to do so, ponder the implications on a personal level for a moment…

→ **Q:** What's your natural impulse when you see someone following you in hot pursuit?

→ **A:** You skedaddle.

And that's what your prospective customers, clients, and patients will do once they see you chasing after them—and no matter what kind of shape you're in, they can outrun and outlast you. You will wind up left in their dust… undoubtedly along with the rest of your fellow competitors, because it's almost certain they don't know any better either.

I recommend a different approach. Stop chasing. Start magnetically attracting. Lay out something they would value as "bait" to magnetically attract them and that will cause them to take notice and request information from you. This "bait" could be as simple as a two-page report promising to solve a specific problem they face or a free consumer report guide. (You do this based on your research and how well you understand them.)

This idea of having "them come to you" flips everything around and changes the game. Using this kind of approach, where you offer something of value for free in exchange for getting someone to step forward, raise his/her hand, and say "I'm interested in learning more" gives you the opportunity to separate yourself from the competition and it completely reverses the power position of who's chasing whom.

When you stop chasing, you no longer have to resort to gimmicks to set yourself apart from the pack of hungry competitors running alongside you—like slashing your prices, or grouponing specials—they are magnetically attracted to you.

When you use attraction, this allows you to charge and collect premium fees. People pay more for a solution that they've already at least partially embraced, or better yet—asked for.

Attraction brings to you clients who are more committed and likely to remain with you over the long term. Another benefit is that customers who come to you through attraction are naturally inclined to remain with you and do business with you over and again.

Attraction also builds trust, which is a key to making sales in our exceedingly skeptical age. The customer attraction system in *Magnetic Marketing* establishes your credibility and authority by delivering the results—initially on a small scale—exactly as promised, laying the foundation for even bigger sales and greater trust as you continue to deliver real value.

Attraction enables you to sell exactly what they want to buy because it ONLY draws in prospects who fit your criteria and mindset. You know them inside out, you know what they want, you attract them with something that you know works, and they'll buy and keep buying.

So what kind of marketer do you want to be? Constantly chasing after people who may or may not want you? Or calmly waiting and watching as eager, new prospects knock on your door and ask for the help only you can provide.

MISTAKE #7: THINKING YOU HAVE THE AD BUDGET OF COCA-COLA

It's only natural to think the advertising you should emulate is what you see every day on TV. Because that's where the big ad dollars get spent and by the biggest, most respected brands in business like GE, GM, Google, Apple, Microsoft, Kellogg's, Anheuser-Busch, and Coca-Cola.

Millions pour into the coffers of ad agencies to produce high-definition, high-dollar commercials for the itching eyeballs of the nation. With these ads, they hope to move us emotionally, to make us laugh, and to make us associate their brands with happy feelings so that when the time comes to make a relevant buying decision, we choose them.

That's the game they're playing. And the cost to join them at the table is enormous. Most small businesses have nothing even remotely close to the ad budgets of these companies. In 2017, Coca-Cola's advertising expenses were $3.96 Billion.

Do you really want to play that game too? You're not Coca-Cola. You're not going after every parched throat on the planet. You don't need to copy what they do with your advertising.

You need to do what works for you.

MISTAKE #8: RACE TO THE BOTTOM IN LOW PRICE

When you don't have a real system in place to market your products or services, you tend to look at what your competitors are doing to build up their businesses and nine times out of ten it's lower prices.

This occurs in practically every industry, every marketplace from ice cream to IT. A mad dash to the bottom in the hopes that lower prices will give you the edge you need.

The only problem with this is the simple fact that there can only be ONE lowest-priced offering. Someone's got to take the hit to be number one in that race. But pole position is easy to come by, especially if you have deep pockets and you don't care if you lose money over the short term. You can afford to drive the competitors out of business.

Then congratulations, you're King.

Until you're not.

Bottom dwelling is NOT the path to long term success.

MISTAKE #9: THERE'S NO FOLLOW UP

I see this all the time and—even though I know better than to invest any emotional energy into the exercise—it still drives me crazy.

The wife and I decide to go out to eat. We always eat at a few tried and true establishments, but what the heck, let's try someplace different.

So we head into town and see a new restaurant has just opened up. It looks okay from the outside, the parking lot isn't full, but it isn't empty either, so we decide to give it a try.

We go in, get seated, the server arrives and asks for drinks and then our order. Food arrives, it's actually better than expected. There's a nice dessert menu, followed by some coffee (equally good), and then the check, a tip, and out the door.

Overall, a relatively pleasant, enjoyable experience from start to finish.

That was our perception.

But we'll probably NEVER return.

Why? Because they didn't seem to even notice we even existed.

Sure, all the basic functions of a restaurant were executed properly—wait staff, food service, cooking, accounting, and so forth.

But they missed the ONE thing that could make or break their business.

They put zero effort into doing everything they could to make sure of our return.

There was no capture of name, address, even email.

There was no offer of a bounce-back coupon to entice us to come back.

They didn't ask about our anniversary, our birthdays, children, friends, none of that.

ZERO effort went into knowing us as anything but an ephemeral visitor out of the blue who showed up one night and then passed like a ship out to sea, never to been heard from or seen again.

Tragic.

THE ANSWER IS SIMPLE

When you truly know your WHO, you can magnetically attract all the clients, customers, and patients you can handle. And you don't have to do this by slashing your prices, chasing after everyone in hopes of catching someone, or spending yourself into oblivion trying to imitate massive multinationals with marketing budgets greater than half the world's GDP.

You can't afford to make any of these mistakes and you don't have to—because it's not about you, it's about them. Knowing them and their needs inside and out and then meeting them exactly where they live with just what they've been looking for.

Getting the right Message—via the right Media—to the right Market—it all starts with knowing your WHO.

CHAPTER 3

What Happens When You Attract Instead of Chase?

If you run a business, whether it's behind the counter at a walk-in location or you're sitting in your home office beside the phone, the worst feeling in the world is the same:

Silence.

Without a constant flow of leads and customers coming to your business, you're doomed to fail.

It doesn't matter how good you are, how motivated you are, how wonderful your products/services are, none of that matters. The lifeblood of every business is LEADS and CUSTOMERS and the beauty of *Magnetic Marketing* is that you don't have to suffer in silence any longer—nor do you have to experience the pain of chasing them down via the painful path of "cold calling."

Instead, you allow your SYSTEM to magnetically attract them to you—prequalified, prescreened, and already interested in you and what you have to offer.

And don't let the word "SYSTEM" scare you. What you'll discover in this book is simple to understand and straightforward to implement, even if you don't have any kind of technology background.

It's all about NOT chasing customers anymore, it's about ATTRACTING them instead by:

→ Abandoning strategies that everyone else is using that just don't work.

→ Making MARKETING your business and your message your #1 priority.

→ Focusing your marketing on the needs and dreams of the customers you want to magnetically attract.

The difference can be dramatic, as you'll see in these stories of business owners like you who switched from marketing like everyone else and instead took that first step to implementing *Magnetic Marketing* principles for themselves.

"CHANGING MY MESSAGE CHANGED MY BUSINESS."

Derek Emery owns one of the largest independent used car buying services in the state of California, but it took him ten years to discover the secret that would exponentially grow his business. After embracing the principles of *Magnetic Marketing*, Derek realized that people selling their cars were not just looking for a professional used car buying service, they were really looking for a bank.

When he understood this, he completely revamped his USP accordingly: "Not only will we buy someone's used car, but we will guarantee cash in hand in twenty minutes or less."

That small little USP tripled his business overnight. People started seeing his company as a quick way to acquire cash—not just sell a car.

With this knowledge, he was able to position his company as not just a source of power in the marketplace; he became the ONLY source of power in the marketplace. He was able to develop the right message to the right market, using the right multiple sources of media.

Before *Magnetic Marketing*, his company was buying and selling two hundred to three hundred cars a month. With the *Magnetic Marketing* changes, he is constantly buying and selling over one thousand cars a month. Most of the cars he is now buying now are the profitable cars. He no longer has to buy the "traditional junk car."

He was able to get the right customer, the right car, and the most amount of profit by implementing the principles of *Magnetic Marketing*.

"BEING GREAT WAS NO BETTER THAN LOUSY WITHOUT PATIENTS TO PRESENT GREAT TO."

Dr. Dustin Burleson opened his dental practice in 2006 with the thinking that *"you get your degree, do good work, and like the Field of Dreams, the patients will come."*

As he quickly discovered, that's not how the real world works. For the first three years he grew his business through blood, sweat, and tears. But he soon felt stuck.

Looking for ways to escape the hamster wheel and build a better business, Dr. Burleson stumbled upon a book I wrote that opened his eyes to the power of *Magnetic Marketing*. After consuming that book, he had a key revelation ... he wasn't in the business of being an orthodontist, he was actually in the business of MARKETING orthodontic services. If he didn't devote dedicated time to creating a system to magnetically attract patients to his practice—he would never achieve the practice he had dreamed of.

The cold hard truth is that it doesn't matter how good you are. You could be the best lawyer, the best dentist, or the best orthodontist in the world. But if you can't get the message out to the public, no one will ever get a chance to experience how wonderful you are.

His practice has gone from four chairs in one small clinic to four locations with five orthodontists, and from one employee to thirty-five employees. He spends time with the local college giving real world entrepreneurial advice, and has even created his own coaching programs to help other orthodontists!

"MY BUSINESS CHANGED WHEN I STOPPED DOING WHAT EVERYONE ELSE WAS DOING."

Dave Dee was stuck in a job he hated, working long hours scraping by to support his family, while all the while he had dreams of becoming a professional magician. Like many small business owners working to create a career on the side, he was really good at what he did, but he knew nothing about marketing other than doing the same thing other magicians were doing and hoping for referrals.

His fledgling side business was working out as well as you might expect—he was only doing about three shows a month and these weren't big corporate extravaganzas with big corporate checks. These were children's birthday parties and even though he excelled in this, the inability to create any kind of regular, predictable stream of business meant he couldn't generate anywhere near enough money to go off on his own with any assurance he could still pay the bills.

Then without warning—he was fired from his day job. Already deep in debt, he grew frustrated and angry, knowing that something had to change and fast.

Almost by chance, he attended a SUCCESS event of ten thousand people and encountered a message he'd never heard of before from the very last speaker of the day, me.

The message was simple:

STOP doing what everyone else is doing, trying to chase business using the same ads, the same tactics as all your competitors. Instead, leverage proven principles to magnetically attract the very best clients to you.

Dave realized that this was the answer to finally living his dream of becoming a professional magician—he knew is his gut that *Magnetic Marketing* was the key to the vault.

On the very same day my program arrived, he literally locked himself in a room over Friday, Saturday and Sunday and went through the entire *Magnetic Marketing System and Toolkit*.

Then, on Monday, he started implementing the customer attraction strategies.

It was like a miracle. In less than ninety days, Dave went from doing three shows a month to averaging more than thirty shows a month! In his fourth month, he did fifty-seven shows!

He was living the dream. Everything changed!

His wife was able to quit both of her jobs and he paid off all his credit card debt. He bought a new home, a new car, and finally had financial freedom for the first time in his entire life.

"WENT FROM STRUGGLING TO MASSIVE SUCCESS WITH LEAD GENERATION."

Ben Glass is a personal injury attorney who (twenty years ago) had just left the comforts of a law firm to start his own practice. So he does what seems natural—look around at what other lawyers are doing and copy what they do. But nothing seemed to make the phone ring.

He came across my best-selling training *The Magnetic Marketing System and Toolkit* (I didn't have a book like this at that time). The concept of lead generation marketing jumped out at him. He then understood that there was a simple process to get people interested in his business and a system for marketing directly to those people.

He didn't fully understand the power of Magnetic Marketing when he started, he just started following the system. But boy, did it pay off in spades.

He now has one of the most successful practices in his area, where he went from struggling to get clients to a predictable system that delivers clients on a daily basis. Today, he is a father of nine, grandfather of two, an active soccer referee, and respected thought leader who continues to break the molds in his highly regulated industry.

THE PROOF IS IN THE PUDDING...

I'll acknowledge, there're so many people running around touting the next big thing that it's become harder to know who to listen to and who to trust.

As they say, the proof lies in the pudding.

These stories represent just the tip of the iceberg representing literally thousands of lives changed for entrepreneurs and business owners of all shapes and sizes since the first version of *Magnetic*

Marketing was released over twenty-five years ago.

The difference to their businesses was dramatic—all because they made the shift from "Chasing Customers" to "Attracting Customers."

Even though some of the specific examples used have changed due to new forms of media emerging, the foundational principles remain solidly in place and continue to run like clockwork—attracting slam-dunk customers, patients, or clients to your business.

And the good news is that with the ever-expanding number of media options now available, it's never been easier to put together a *Magnetic Marketing* system customized perfectly for YOU.

Note: Now you might be saying to yourself, *"But wait, my business is different ... what if I am in the commodity business? I HAVE to price my services lower than anyone else in order to get the business I need."*

First off, your business is NOT different. Every industry faces the pressure to lower prices, as one of the easiest ways to differentiate yourself in the marketplace is to announce yourself as the lowest priced option.

If this is the route you choose to follow, I wish you the best. But understand, it's only a matter of time before someone else emerges to go after your customers with an even lower priced option. Then you'll be forced to either lose those customers or instead compete in a downward spiral to oblivion. It's a race very few can win and almost never for long.

The beauty of *Magnetic Marketing* lies in the way it sets YOU apart from the competition in a way that's focused on features/benefits you control—and that make you a UNIQUE solution to the challenges your perfect customer faces. In essence, you eliminate price as the key component in the buying...

...decision and in reality, most buyers place price lower than other factors to be considered, such as convenience, quality, guarantee, and so on.

Magnetic Marketing frees you from the danger of relying on pricing alone to make the sale. Even in industries where there's significant price pressure, it's almost dead certain that customers exist to pay you what your worth.

All you have to do is identify and magnetically attract them.

Emilio Couret

From Stagnant to Thriving

How Emilio Couret DDS Turned his Dental Practice Around in One Year Using Info-First Marketing

Emilio Couret was extremely frustrated. He didn't know what to do, and he didn't have a plan.

He'd dreamed of owning a small business from the time he was a 7-year-old boy pumping gas at his dad's gas stations. He'd invested thirteen years getting ready to open his own business: Four years getting a business degree at Indiana University, another four at the University of Iowa Dental School, and five years working at his mentor's dental practice.

When he opened his own practice, Dente Complete Dentistry (mydente.com), in 2006, he believed what he'd been told --that his hard work and dedication to the highest level of service would bring in business. "I felt like if you're a good dentist, you just throw your shingle up and people would just come in," Emilio said. "I found out that was not true."

So, he did what many businesses do. He invested more money and time. "I began hiring people that claimed they were experts," Emilio recalls, "and I threw away a lot of money to the people promising me all these new patients that I was going to be attracting. None of it came true." After owning his practice for ten years and not getting the results he wanted, he decided to learn how to do his own marketing. While listening to podcasts to educate himself,

he repeatedly heard Dan Kennedy's name mentioned. He began buying Dan's books and reading them cover to cover.

In the year and a half since discovering Dan Kennedy and Magnetic Marketing, Emilio has done massive implementation which is quickly and drastically changing the landscape of his business.

While only increasing his marketing budget by 2%, he has gone from zero growth month after month to attracting 20 new patients per month and a 22% increase in revenue.

Discovering Why His Marketing Wasn't Working

In reading Dan Kennedy's books, *No B.S. Direct Marketing for Non-Direct Marketing Businesses*, and *The Ultimate Marketing Plan*, Emilio made his first big discoveries...

1) Stop emulating big dumb companies. "The way I was looking at marketing was the same way McDonald's does marketing or Coca-Cola does marketing," Emilio said, "You just kind of throw it out there and flood the market with stuff... this wasn't working because I didn't have the money to do that."

2) Get the message out and let people know what you do. It wasn't just

Reprinted from the NO B.S. Marketing Letter September 2018

getting the message out to attract new patients, it was also letting his existing patients know what he did. "A lot of patients didn't know I do cosmetic work because it hadn't come up," Emilio said. "People would come in for a checkup and they didn't know I had those other services, so they aren't going to spend that extra money with me."

3) Learn the math. One thing which made a significant impact on Emilio's business is learning to "do the math." Before Magnetic Marketing, Emilio didn't have a good tracking system in place, nor a good grasp on things such as the lifetime value of his patients. Doing the math is helping him hold his marketing accountable and create a realistic picture of his business so he can make better decisions.

Plug the Holes First

"The first thing I noticed was that I was getting 15 new patients a month, but my practice hadn't grown, it was stagnant," Emilio said. "I did the math and if nobody's leaving and I'm adding 15 new patients a month, I should be flooded. I realized as quickly as they were coming in, they were leaving."

Emilio's first step was to plug up holes internally by making a personal connection with his patients. He used several info-marketing strategies to fence in his herd. These included:

A monthly printed newsletter: "The companies doing newsletters on a massive level for dentists focused the content on all scientific things," Emilio said. "They were kind of boring to read." Magnetic Marketing resources recommended the newsletter should be more personal, with only about 25% of the content about things like gum disease. He received immediate positive feedback after mailing his newsletter. "I had patients come in and say, "Oh, I love the story about you and your son going on the train and I love the story about your dad," Emilio said. "People would talk about it and people began sharing it with their friends."

Daily emails: Wanting to immerse himself in the principles he was learning from Magnetic Marketing, he joined Peak Performers. During one of the Peak meetings, Dave Dee talked about how he does daily emails for his customers. "Dave gave us the formula of how to do it," Emilio recalled, "It would be something that happened to you personally that week and then tied into how that related to your business." Emilio confessed that some were skeptical about a daily email from their dentist and told him not to do it, but he did it anyway. Injecting his personality, he writes daily emails which he also posts on his Facebook page. "I write them on Sunday and on Monday we plug them in and they go out every day at the same time at 8:00 AM," Emilio said. Emilio's patients love his daily emails. They tell him they are not only reading them daily but forwarding them to friends and family.

Shock and awe welcome packages: Emilio sends out a welcome package to every new patient. The package includes a welcome card thanking them for being a new patient, a report titled: The Top Ten Things You Should Know Before You Choose Your Dentist, his new book Achieve The Ultimate Dental Experience and a list of testimonials.

Next, Create A Reward System That Fuels Referrals

At another Peak meeting, Emilio was asked where he got most of his patients. When he said referrals, he was instructed to beef up his referral system since that was what was working. Emilio did this by:

Creating rewards to get people talking: To get people talking about him more, he changed the gifts he was offering for referrals. "When anybody refers a patient to us, the first thing we do is send them brownies to their work," Emilio said. "This gets people talking about us. Then if they send another person, then we send them flowers if it's a woman, or we will buy pizza for everybody at their job."

Rewarding loyalty & top spenders: Emilio previously gave gifts to new patients. "The patients that were with you forever and had been super loyal never get anything," Emilio said, "I'm doing the opposite now." Emilio gives long-term patients $25 restaurant gift cards when they come in to get their teeth cleaned. Patients who spend a lot of money with him or refer a ton of people, receive a bottle of wine.

Keeping the referral system top of mind: From reading Dan's book, *No B.S. Guide to Maximum Referrals and Customer Retention*, Emilio got the idea to donate $25 to charity each time someone refers a new patient. "I donate $25 to this place called Infant Welfare Society, which is a community dental clinic that provides free to heavily discounted dental care to kids," Emilio said. "We also put in our newsletter, "This month we were able to help 1020 kids thanks to your referrals." Emilio also lists all new patients that come in during the month.

Third, Use Info-FIRST Marketing To Attract New Patients

Once Emilio had systems in place to stop the leaks, he began using Magnetic Marketing strategies to attract new patients. While these systems are relatively new, Emilio is already seeing a consistent 33% bump in the number of patients he is attracting each month. Emilio predicts this to have a significant impact on his bottom line since the lifetime value of a patient is $5,000.00. Here's a look at what he did:

Segmented messaging on his website: Emilio looked at the different reasons people come to his office and created separate messaging for each group. "There are basically five reasons," Emilio said, "And you have to talk differently to those people. For example, you talk differently to the person who is afraid of the dentist than to the person who is coming in for a cosmetic consultation."

Info-FIRST marketing: Emilio created a free report called, The Top Ten Things You Should Know Before You Choose Your Dentist. He also wrote a book called: Achieve The Ultimate Dental Experience which he published in May 2018. Available on his website and Amazon, Emilio's book showcases how his practice differs from other dental providers. It includes chapters such as "Eliminate Dental Anxiety in Minutes," and "Achieve the Smile of Your Dreams in One Day."

"The book is divided into seven different objections that people have when they go to the dentist," Emilio explained. "Like they're afraid of the needle ... they want to get as much done in one appointment as possible ... and that's basically how I wrote it, to address those objections."

He added a blog to his website as well as educational videos that give tips every week on topics such as "Why does my tooth hurt when I chew," brushing, flossing, sensitive teeth and so on.

The Final Word: Emilio's next goal is to scale his business. When asked what keeps him motivated to implement so much Emilio says two things: #1 is his family. "I want to ramp up my business so that I'm making money when I'm not there, so I can spend more time with them," Emilio said. #2 is continually learning. "When you're a business owner, you feel like you're alone and nobody understands you. You're scared sometimes," Emilio continues, "It motivates me to hear these guys. A lot of them have been through the same stuff and you don't feel alone anymore. You get motivated. You can walk into the office with some energy."

CHAPTER 4

What This Actually Looks Like

Marketing is often viewed as a mysterious but necessary evil, as in *"it's definitely not the business, it's something I have to soil myself with in order to make my business work."*

You are here because you are willing to reconsider that entire paradigm. It makes you a rare bird soon to take flight way above all others.

The need for more leads and more customers for lifeblood exists in businesses of all shapes and sizes, but few business owners ever develop formal, organized marketing systems to meet this need.

Instead, they constantly seek out the one magic bullet that will solve this problem—SEO, pay-per-click, social media, TV, billboards, radio, print ads—they hope that someone will provide the answer.

The biggest mistake made is they immediately focus on the media without having a plan or a system in mind first. They are often sold media and pour money into redoing all their websites or making new videos for them, into buying online traffic, into some "one thing" to change everything.

I call these random and erratic acts disconnected investments in attempted marketing.

You need to realize that most ad agencies and most media representatives have a great understanding and reliance upon of what's called "image" or "institutional" advertising.

It's what I call Goodyear blimp advertising.

When Goodyear flies a blimp over a stadium, they don't have any illusion that at half-time of the football game, thirty-five thousand people are going to jump up out of their seats and run out and buy snow tires. They don't expect that to happen and it's a good thing they don't because obviously it doesn't.

What they're hoping for and what they're buying is that, over a long period of time, by these sports fans seeing the Goodyear blimp over and again, they connect it with this happy pleasant event and they have warm, nice, fuzzy feelings for Goodyear. Then, someday when they have to go buy a tire, all of that comes together in their mind and causes them to buy a Goodyear tire.

I call that high-risk marketing. It just seems to me that there's a straighter line to get from a person who needs tires to buying Goodyear tires than going through all of that rigmarole of building a blimp and hiring a pilot and finding a football game and flying a blimp over it.

There is—and it's called "Direct Marketing" or "Response-Driven Marketing" or—when integrated into a complete system of attracting and converting leads—"*Magnetic Marketing*."

This approach is derived from what used to be called mail order.

The discipline of the entire mail order industry—now the direct marketing industry—is that for every dollar invested there is a direct, typically fast and always measurable return of that dollar plus presumably some profit. You can boil it down to two very basic ideas:

1.   Spend $1.00 on marketing, get back $2.00 or $20.00, fast, that can be accurately tracked back to the initial $1.00 invested.

2. Do NOT spend $1.00 on any marketing or advertising that does not directly and quickly bring back $2.00 or $20.00.

Go back and reread these two steps. Make sure you fully grasp this life-changing principle. They should affect EVERY action you take from this point forward when it comes to marketing your business.

It's not new and it's almost certain that you've seen, heard, read examples of it on television, radio, letters, and so forth for most if not all of your life. Maybe you have even participated in it, without knowing it.

Most media people and most ad agency people have little or no understanding of that kind of advertising and marketing. Most even fear it because it is so accountable.

To make this system work, however, the first thing you must understand in depth is WHO your customer is. Because even the best possible offer made to someone who is wholly unqualified, or wholly disinterested in it is not going to work. It will fall on deaf ears.

Therefore, you've got to match your offers with precisely the right people.

KNOWING THE WHO IS THE MOST IMPORTANT THING YOU'LL DO

There's a story about legendary copywriter Gary Halbert, who once asked a room of aspiring writers, "Imagine you're opening a hamburger stand on the beach—what do you need most to succeed?" Answers included, "secret sauce," and "great location" and "quality meat." Halbert replied, "You missed the most important thing—A STARVING CROWD."

Your job is to find that "starving crowd" who can't live without what it is you have to offer.

What we want to do in terms of targeting is to find good, prospective customers for our business that can be reached affordably, that are likely to buy, that are able to buy, and preferably who already know of us, or are likely to trust us.

Once you get this down, and you nail exactly who your slam-dunk customer truly is—the person you absolutely want to do business with over and again—then you'll be able to make your marketing "magnetic" because you'll be using words and phrases that'll attract your target audience. This makes your job much easier, because you can talk to them using language they relate to about what it is they really want.

WHAT YOUR WHO REALLY WANTS

Knowing exactly what your perfect customer wants to buy is NOT as simple as it might seem. For example, there's the old story of the guy walking into the hardware store looking for a 3/4" drill bit. The mistake that's easily made is thinking the customer wants a 3/4" inch drill bit.

Wrong. <u>He wants a 3/4" inch hole</u>. The drill bit is just the hoop he has to jump through to get it.

Let's take it a step further than recognizing the "want" for a 3/4" inch hole… what's the underlying need driving THAT desire? Is it simply to hang a picture? Or does our homeowner crave a lifestyle surrounded by elegance that makes their home the envy of family, friends, and coworkers? So it's not just about merely needing a hole, it's about Pride and an increased sense of Self-Worth.

That's a much deeper longing and tapping into THAT is where you want to connect with your WHO. You want to solve their problem, not just sell them something.

It's very easy to get this wrong in your messaging.

For example, you'll see financial planners competing with one another offering "estate plans." Not that there's anything wrong with estate planning, it's a definite need in the minds of many fifty-plus year olds. But compare the phrasing "Looking for an estate plan?" to "Interested in a solution to take care of your family when you're gone?"

That's a much stronger, more emotional way of connecting to the prospective customer using terms and phrasing that resonates to what's going on inside their heads.

Another example might concern a simple service like a children's magician, whose primary market is selling birthday party magic shows to moms. A headline that reads "Joe Blow the Magician" followed by text all about Joe is appealing if "Joe" is world-renowned (not likely). Better messaging would be "Imagine: A Birthday Party Your Child Will Remember and Treasure Forever—Guaranteed!"

That's what Mom really wants. Sorry Joe.

To help you better understand this concept, and how it might affect you and your business, here are fifteen different industries and what their WHO really wants.

1. **Financial Services:** Financial Services can mean a lot of things. Maybe you sell insurance, annuities, or stocks. Or maybe you have the ability to sell a mix of products to serve the needs of your clients. Whatever your particular specialty, in this industry, the name of the game is "**peace.**" What you're really doing is helping people avoid the 3 a.m. sweats.

No one wants to worry about whether they can put their kids through college or becoming a burden to their family when they're old. The idea of running out of money with life left to live is downright frightening.

If you're at the higher end of service in this niche and serving the ultra-wealthy, you too are providing peace. It's a different kind of peace, of course. It's the kind that results in knowing that all of their work and investments won't be washed away by a few bad economic cycles. Those folks would like to know that they've provided true generational wealth for their grandkids. In addition to selling your own expertise and trust-worthiness, your target market needs to believe that YOU have the ultimate solution to their 3 a.m. sweats problem ... that their PEACE is what your business is all about.

2. **Insurance:** There are variables in this industry depending on the type of insurance you sell. But in all cases, as the name suggests, you are selling **peace of mind**. Don't think this is a luxury people won't invest in. They want to sleep well at night knowing that the worst-case scenario will NOT happen to them because they have you. **They want peace** and aside from talking about the particulars of great rates, service, etc., people are yearning for you to show them that with you, they can finally stop worrying.

3. **Legal:** In the legal industry, no matter what particular niche you serve, the number one thing you're selling is **advocacy**. People need to know that someone they can trust is in THEIR corner. They need someone on their side.

   So, if you represent men in divorce and custody battles, oftentimes you may be the ONLY person who is on their side that they can trust. And this holds true in every legal niche … taxes, personal injury, estate law, family, bankruptcy.

   People might say they want to pay less in taxes (of course they do), that they want custody of their kids (hopefully, they do), etc. But what they really want is to know that they've got someone in their corner, fighting for the best possible outcome for them.

   It's a lonely world out there. People need an expert like you to be on their team when they're going through tough times or preparing for the future.

4. **Health & Wellness:** There's a lot to sell in the health and wellness industry and so much of it can be surface level stuff that's obvious. Focusing on the obvious won't get you the deep connection you need to solidify your relationship with your market. Yes, we all want a sexy body, a longer life, energy, a healthier heart, body, and mind. And some of those things are really deep and personal.

But if you go deeper, you'll see that what people really want as it relates to health and wellness is **confidence**. So in this industry, confidence is the REAL thing you're selling. Sometimes we're talking about deep down confidence and the comfort in your own skin that comes from being fit and strong.

Sometimes it's the confidence you feel from knowing that you're fueling your body with the best nutrition available. And sometimes the confidence you're selling is about having the confidence to know that you're fit enough to walk around an amusement park with your children.

With the internet at our fingertips and a constantly changing narrative from health experts, people are easily confused. What they need most from you is confidence that if they buy from you or work with you to achieve their goal, they're doing the right thing for themselves or for their families and that they will be able to achieve that goal.

5. **Chiropractic:** There are obviously a lot of different niches you could serve in this industry. But, let's say for a moment that you serve the elderly demographic. You might think that they just want to be able to play a little more golf or keep up with their grandkids. Those things might be true and they'll certainly admit to them.

But if you go deeper, you'll find that **they want to be the envy of all of their friends who are falling apart.** That's the secret ego motivation that inspires them to find you. And further, they do NOT want to be put into a nursing home. That's the secret fear that has them searching for you. Sell them abilities their friends don't have and you'll have them eating out of your hand.

6. **Dentistry:** There are two big things people REALLY want from their dentist. They will usually tell you about the first thing but not the second. First, they don't want to feel a thing. Even people who don't have a dramatic fear of the dentist share this desire. Dentists are associated with pain for good reason and mouth pain is the worst. This fear of pain is deep and real for just about everyone on planet Earth so it needs your attention. But what they really come to you for is **confidence**. This is the thing that they usually won't say out loud. Men and women alike just want to feel attractive. They want to feel confident when they speak and smile. So while you must address the pain issue, **what people are willing to put their fears aside for is the possibility that you can give them a smile they can be proud of.** Sell that deep down confidence.

7. **Fitness:** Much the same as the health and wellness industry, in fitness, you're selling much more than a sexy body or healthy heart. What

people really want is to believe that they can be a version of themselves that has only ever been imaginary up until this point. They want to believe that it's possible to be that person ... the person who feels incredibly confident about the way he or she looks and rightfully so. That's who you can help them be. *Keep in mind that mentioning the work involved with this achievement is a turnoff.* People want to believe that they can easily, magically, transform into their best self. Sell that transformation.

8. **Service Business:** Why choose one plumber over another? Or, why choose one landscaper, babysitter, tutor, contractor, or mechanic over another one out there? Again, this will vary depending on the service you provide. But a lot of this comes down to consistently showing people that you want the business and backing up that demonstration with consistently excellent service, **the kind of treatment that you'd give your own mother.**

No one wants to hire the guy who wants the work. We all want to hire the guy who would be glad to fit us in and take a look and then takes us under his wing and tells us that we've been spending too much and he has a cheaper solution or that our tires will actually last another eighteen months. We want someone to show us that we can count on them to take good care of us.

9. **Sales:** Sales is a broad industry and what people REALLY want depends on what you sell. But if you're up against three other suits and you're all making the same offer, always remember that the winner is usually the person who puts extra time and effort into the relationship. What does that tell us about what people *really* want? They want to feel like you care about helping them. They want to feel like you are excited about earning their business. **They REALLY want to feel important.**

10. **Real Estate:** A lot like the legal profession, people want an advocate. So they need to know that YOU are in THEIR corner. Real estate is one of those fields where the laws are different everywhere and always changing. The confusion makes it such that the average citizen cannot properly advocate for himself or herself. They need an expert. And while they may say that they want to get a great price, **what they REALLY want is an expert in their corner fighting for them.** You are *really* selling that hero.

11. **Retail:** Assuming you sell clothes, people want much more than deep discounts, great service, and a great selection. These are the things they'll tell you they want. But what they won't say is that they want to walk out of your store feeling like the most fashionable, attractive, "together" version of themselves. If you sell suits to men, they want

to walk out feeling "like a man" who commands respect! If you sell casual clothes to women, they want to walk out feeling like they can take on the world looking amazing, no matter what life throws at them. **It's about transformation.** Your marketing needs to address the transformation, not just the discounts or other details.

12. **Automotive:** If you own a repair shop, what your customers *really* want will be different than if you sell detailing services. So it's important to know your market. But assuming you're in the repair business-people will outright tell you that they don't want to be ripped off and they want to preserve the investment they've made in their vehicle.

    But what they secretly want is to never have to come into your shop for service. And when they do, **they don't want it to disturb their lives at all.** They don't want to feel it. Obviously this is something you can't actually give them. But you can address all of this in your sales copy. You should be using language that talks about how you're in the business of keeping the people in your town in motion for longer because no one wants to slow down to take care of their vehicle.

13. **Restaurant:** There will always be people who come for a free meal or because the fridge is empty, they're short on time, or just didn't plan

dinner. But at the end of the day, people choose a restaurant for a bigger reason than all of these reasons. **What they really want is a positive or memorable experience.** When they imagine where they'll eat tonight, their brains are processing what the experience will be like. Will everyone be in a good mood? Will they have a good time? Yes, some of those things hinge on quality, price, service, and speed. But what you're really selling is a "good time."

14. **Coaching & Consulting:** If you're in the coaching and consulting field, you might think you're selling support, guidance, camaraderie, or a helping hand. But people typically want much more than all of this from their coach or consultant. In fact, they really want to **believe that they already have the ability** within themselves to achieve their goals.

So while what they say they want is success in your area of expertise, what they really want is someone to show them how to bring out the best of themselves and the power already within to achieve their goals. This is true whether you teach yoga, piano, or business success. The key for you to focus on is that whatever they want to achieve in this area, they already are quite capable. Your role is to first show them that they actually do have this power and then to show them how to use it.

15. **Info-marketing:** You may think you're selling specialized knowledge in a particular field, but what you're really selling here is **transformation**.

Let's say you help financial advisors make more money with your info-marketing business ... you may have coaching groups or products to help them succeed in certain aspects of the business, and maybe even some done-for-you elements. At the end of the day, it's not information that they want from you (yes, the name of this industry is deceiving).

What you're really marketing is the life they want for themselves. They want to know that you can help them achieve the transformation they're looking for. That you can help them go from where they are now (A) to where they want to be (B).

If your info-business provides parenting solutions to people with troubled, adopted teens (point A—this is where they are now), you're selling a happy, well-adjusted kid that grows into a loving, productive adult (point B—the transformation they want to achieve).

People want the "dream" and your job is to show them that your products and/or services will be the catalyst for that transformation. And in the case of this parenting info-biz, those parents also have their own selfish, internal motives. They want to know that they are the best parent they can be ... that they're doing everything they possibly can for their child. So in this case, it's transformation plus pride.

As you can tell, there's a lot to truly understanding your WHO and what matters most to them. It requires a lot of careful thought and analysis, but the rewards are well worth it.

Having a solid understanding is only the first step though. Now you need to connect what THEY want with what YOU have to offer. And it all takes shape with a simple triangle...

Member Spotlight:

Jeremy Kezhaya and Dr. Laura Shwaluk

What Is True Business Freedom? How About Taking 4 – 5 Months Off Every Year?

Meet the Magnetic Marketing style entrepreneurial couple who approach business as a formula with exact systems that 'freaking work!'

Breaking a million dollars in 1992, The Auto Shop, Plano Texas, is a multimillion-dollar car repair shop in an industry where their average competitor only does $350,000 a year.

The alone would be reason to take notice.

> **"It's about having a business you created to provide you the freedom and income. Not just creating a job for yourself."**

However, husband and wife team Jerry Kezhaya and Dr. Laura Shwaluk have not one, but six highly profitable businesses. In addition to The Auto Shop, they own and run the multi-million dollar Express Exterior Car Wash business, the 7-figure chiropractor business NTC Health and Fitness, and a 100% occupied retail shopping center, which when purchased, was only 11 percent occupied. They also own the Texas Wine Posse, which Jerry describes as "a hobby out of control." In addition to wine accessories, they bottle their own wine. And their most recent passion, which quickly grew to six figures in just two years, is their Business Builders Mentor and Mastermind, a coaching and mentoring group

teaching business owners how to own a business that gives true freedom.

Even more impressive is that Jerry and Laura have done more than make a lot of money. They've discovered how to create real freedom taking an impressive four to five months off a year, every year, for the last four years. With one business that would be incredible; multiply that by six businesses, and we're sure you'll agree, it makes sense to pay attention to every word they have to say.

"What allows us to do that, is that business is a formula," says Laura. "When you have the formula in place, the systems in place, then you don't have to be at the business." A big part of that formula has been implementing Magnetic Marketing principles. A fundamental core of every business is to be completely different from what everybody else is doing. What separates The Auto Shop from every other repair business is that they do not pay their people commission and prevent the consumer from being charged for unnecessary repairs.

> **"We regurgitate Magnetic Marketing in all of our marketing with our clients because it freaking works."**

Reprinted from the NO B.S. Marketing Letter October 2017

"In the typical shop, whether it's a dealership or a franchise store, everybody is paid a piece of what you spend," says Jerry; "I think that just rigs the system so totally famously against the consumer."

Doing the Right Thing, Whether Required or Not

Jerry and Laura find that doing what's good for the environment is also good for the bottom line.

In Texas, car washes aren't required to have a water reclamation system. But when they their car wash business, Jerry contacted R.W. Harvey, the man contracted by the U.S. federal government to rid nuclear wastewater of heavy metals. Jerry told him, "You and I are going to work together." Two and a half years and several hundred thousand dollars later, they successfully developed a water reclamation system that makes the water so clean that if you run it through carbon, you could drink it. Winning the Environmentalist of The Year for the state of Texas for that reclamation system, today, Jerry and his car wash business use less than three gallons of fresh water when washing a car. (On average, car washes use between 9-45 gallons. Average home wash uses 100 gallons.)

Know Thy Customer

One of the biggest breakthroughs for Jerry and Laura's businesses happened when they understood the importance of an avatar – properly identifying your ideal target market.

"We didn't even know what the hell an avatar was," Jerry recalls. "We didn't know about segmenting our list… We wasted thousands, tens, hundreds of thousands of dollars in ineffective marketing."

Identifying their avatar allowed them to laser-focus their advertising, meaning they could choose media specifically where their customers are and speak to them in their language. Laura adds that once you have that in place, "Test, test, test – and once it's working, leave it alone!"

This principle has allowed them to keep adding pieces to what Jerry calls "the wagon wheel." So robust is their marketing, there are 30 marketing spokes in their wheel for The Auto Shop alone.

"For an auto repair business, this is unheard of," Jerry says.

One of their most popular "spokes" is their newsletter. "When it hits the mailbox, you absolutely know because our phones light up," says Jerry. The newsletter has nothing to do with cars with the exception of three little coupons that announce that month's special.

Here are some other Magnetic Marketing principles Jerry and Laura have folded into their business setting them miles apart from their competition.

There has to be an offer. One of the biggest principles Dan Kennedy has drilled into their heads is, "If there's no offer, don't even bother sending it." When Jerry and Laura started using EDDM® (Every Door Direct Mail from the USPS), they mailed a 12" x 15" postcard to 8,000 people. This one mailing brought in $40,000 worth of auto repair services.

"If there's no offer, it's not called marketing anymore; it's called branding."

Create a trustworthy relationship. Jerry calls into a radio station and talks to the radio announcer on air as part of his radio ads. Jerry told the radio station he wanted to tell a story as part of his "ad." Today, he calls in several times a week. Because Jerry has developed a relationship with the announcer, she now calls him "Uncle Jerry" on air. Laura says, "That immediately created a relationship with listeners... from a client's perspective, it's like, who do they trust? Well, they might trust their uncle on this, so let's call Uncle Jerry."

Demonstrate your Unique Selling Proposition (USP). To demonstrate The Auto Shop's USP of not paying a commission to their employees, Jerry tells stories on the radio show. On a recent show, Jerry said, "You know, here's something about my industry that just flat-out drives me freaking crazy – the worst one came from a local Honda dealership. They brought it in, I'm looking at the paper right here, right now. It's an estimate for $4,457.30. When we got the car up in the air, it didn't need most of it. We fixed this car for $485. $485, not $4,457.30. So listeners, you owe it to yourselves to come into The Auto Shop for a second opinion. Let us tell you what your car really needs. It makes a huge difference when people are not all paid on commission."

The radio segment ends with the radio announcer saying, "That's right, folks. Take your car to Uncle Jerry at The Auto Shop. The shop you can trust. Jupiter Plano Parkway." She reads off the telephone number, and at the end Jerry says, "Beep beep!"

Create a referral system. Laura admits when asked, "What's your referral system?" she had no idea what that was. "I would, on occasion, ask for referrals," she says, but she had no system.

Putting a system in place changed things dramatically. Laura began giving out cards to every single patient at her chiropractic office that basically says, "We know you have people who you run into that have back pain, neck pain, headaches and whatnot. Would you please give them this card on your behalf and have them come to a free seminar?" The free seminar is less off-putting for people who are skeptical about chiropractors. Having a friend recommend them helps, too.

"Once you have them there, getting them involved, you're almost halfway through the sale," she says. Laura gets prospects involved by doing demonstrations where every single person comes up as a volunteer. Originally, to increase participation, rewards were offered to patients who referred someone. She can no longer do that due to changing regulations; however, she still has a system. If you are unsure about what you can do in your referral system, "Ask your ethics people about whether you can give something in exchange or do a drawing," Laura recommends.

Reprinted from the NO B.S. Marketing Letter October 2017

PRINCIPLES OF MAGNETIC MARKETING

CHAPTER 5

The Magnetic Marketing Triangle

Now let's get to building your *Magnetic Marketing* system. It has three big building blocks, each of which you can imagine as one side of a triangle:

→ **Message**: A truly compelling, preferably irresistible, marketing message.

→ **Market:** High-probability target marketing that identifies only those most likely to respond.

→ **Media:** The most appropriate, effective combination of media used to deliver your message to your market.

These three can't be placed in any kind of sequential order, because no single one is more important than the other and none of them can function without the others. It is a closed triangle. Each feeds the others and when they work together it gives you enormous marketing power.

BUT you can render the triangle powerless if you get any one or more of them wrong.

For example, you can deliver the right message to the right market, but if you use the wrong media, they will never get the message nor have a chance to act on it.

Or, if you get the media and market right, but fall down when it comes to message—the right people will get what you have to say, it's just not going to connect in the way it should.

Finally, the right message via the right media goes out to the world loud and clear—but there's nobody out there to listen.

You must get ALL three right.

This is why it's so important that you really understand each and how they must work.

MARKET

In the previous chapter, I talked about the need to find your "starving crowd" of slam-dunk customers. The idea of NOT going after every human who still has a pulse is probably a somewhat newer concept for many small businesses. In fact, most are probably guilty of "throw mud against the wall" marketing where you are just putting a marketing message out there and hoping that somehow the right people are going to see it or hear it.

With *Magnetic Marketing*, we use a very different approach. Our approach is designed to do one very important thing, and that is eliminate waste to the greatest degree possible. And to eliminate waste, we must narrow our marketing focus to only the people most likely to buy what we have to offer.

The basic way that most people choose their target market is

GEOGRAPHIC. If you have a local business, you may say your customers, clients, or patients come from a ten-mile radius around your business. Some people don't get any more sophisticated in targeting than that.

Targeting with only geographic information is like getting in a plane and dropping flyers and hoping one hits the right person. That may be an exaggeration, but the truth is that, with just some simple tweaks, you can make your geographic target marketing much more effective.

DEMOGRAPHIC information is about how old people are, how much money they have, whether they are married or single, liberal or conservative, what religion they are and so forth.

That's another way to define further who your ideal customer is—and you need to do this—but again it's very surface level. Geographic and demographic information is important, but we want to go even deeper than that.

PSYCHOGRAPHICS delves even deeper because it explains "why" people buy. It includes information like habits, hobbies, spending habits and values.

Demographics and psychographics will allow you to create your ideal customer profile—a detailed picture of people you would like to work with now and in the future. So how do you determine psychographics of your target market? Here are some questions to ask yourself:

→ **What keeps them awake at night, staring at the ceiling, unable to fall asleep as it relates to your product or service?**

→ **What are they frustrated about?**

→ What is causing them pain, right now, as it relates to your product or service?

→ What is the single biggest problem that you can solve for them?

→ What do they secretly, privately desire most?

The last question is very important. For example, most people who sell marketing courses always talk about making more money and getting more customers, clients, and patients—they think THAT is the core desire for many people. But there's a deeper reason—for them and for everyone.

How do you determine your market's secret and private desires? If you've been in your business for a while and you think about it, you are going to come up with what it is, because you know them. It helps if you think about a current or past customer, client, or patient you would love to "clone" if possible.

If not, if you are just getting into a target market, one of the easiest things that you can do is go to online discussion groups and forums. Start reading what people are posting. You will be able to figure out what pain they have just by going. You will be able to see what they secretly, privately desire most.

Immerse yourself in their world. Get their trade magazines and read them. Go to their trade shows. Talk with them. Ask questions. Watch, listen, and read what they say to their peers, how they talk about their lives and what brings meaning and what causes pain. Do what you can to get inside their heads until their deepest needs and dreams become evident to you.

If you've been in their business, walked in their shoes, laughed and cried with them, then you'll begin to understand what they secretly, privately desire most.

And once you've done all this, you'll know your WHO.

MESSAGE

The next building block then is the right message, as in:

What do you say to your marketplace, to your past, present and future prospects, clients and customers that is compelling, that is magnetic, that cannot be ignored, that must be responded to, that draws them to you like a bright porch light on a dark night draws moths?

Do you have a great marketing message? Most businesses don't. A person opens a restaurant, a flower shop, a dental or law practice, a service business, etc. and the message is, "We're open for business."

A marketing message is a way of concisely and clearly saying to the right market, "Here's what I'm all about and here's why you should choose me."

So you need to ask yourself, "What am I going to say to the marketplace and why is what I say going to be interesting and appealing to the marketplace?"

Back in Chapter 1, we talked about the need to identify and create your business's *Unique Selling Proposition* or *USP*. The example I gave was Domino's Pizza, who built their empire based on this USP: "*Fresh hot pizza delivered in thirty minutes or less, guaranteed.*"

You can go out to the market with a USP like this and you'll almost certainly do far better than most of your competitors, who are probably relying on clichés stating "the best" or "number one" or something equally meaningless.

But I'm going to take you a step deeper regarding promotional messaging—into the creation of special, highly appealing offers that I call "*Widgets.*"

WHAT'S A WIDGET?

We call these very special offers *"Widgets"* and the best way to think of it is an offer on steroids.

Let's say, you own a hotel. A common offer might be: "Get 10 percent off your hotel room rate."

A **widget**, however, ups the ante by tossing in extra elements to make it even more attractive, hard to resist, and impossible to compare against competitors. You can think of widgets as packages of services and goods and premiums and experiences bundled together, given a clever name, and promoted as a special, one-of-a-kind buying opportunity. So now, instead of creating an offer like:

"Get 10 percent off your hotel room rate."

Which is frankly pretty boring and easy to ignore, you'll see:

Your Ultimate Weekend of Food and Fun for only $xxx!

- **10 percent savings on regular two-night room rate**
- **Free gourmet dinner for two, both nights**
- **Complimentary bottle of champagne when you arrive**
- **Limo Service from and to the airport—no charge**
- **Eighteen holes of golf for two plus cart**
- **Movie tickets for two, plus popcorn to boot**
- **Limited availability, reserve your spot before midnight tomorrow**

Now that's hard to ignore, especially when presented to the right person at the right time with the right media.

Widget-making is an important marketing skill. Once you've got it, you'll use it regularly and every day in your business. That's why it's so critical to understand the concept.

On a simple level, if we go back to the pizza business as an example, their widget of the week may be themed for the NBA Playoffs. It could include two pizzas plus a liter of Coke and four side salads—all for a special, one-time only low price.

They're not just saying, "Come and buy pizza from us."

They're saying, *"Come in now to get the* **NBA Playoffs Party Dinner Deal**. *"*

THAT special deal is their widget, which so long as the playoffs continue they can promote via email, flyers, TV ads, newspapers, phone scripts, on and on.

One of the best examples that I've seen and that I know quite a bit about, comes from Las Vegas in the hotel and casino business, where pretty much everybody offers the same thing, a place to come and lose a lot of money and have a good time doing it with a lot of lights and pretty girls. For decades, that was the business in Las Vegas.

Years ago, an amazing entrepreneur, Bob Stupak, took over the worst and last hotel on the strip. He had to find a very different way to get people to come and stay at that hotel and gamble in that casino.

He didn't have a tremendous amount of money at the time to do advertising and marketing with, so the conventional ways that Las Vegas hotels market themselves was pretty much out for him.

Bob sat down and he turned the hotel business and the casino business in Las Vegas into a very specific widget that he could hold up and people could see and get a grip on, understand, be attracted by, and buy in advance of use.

Let me describe his widget. Ask yourself if you would respond to it presuming you were convinced it was real.

> "Give me $396 and I'll give you two nights, three days in my hotel in one of the deluxe suites. There will be a bottle of champagne waiting for you when you arrive. You can have unlimited drinks the entire time you're here whether you're gambling or not. Even if you're sitting in one of the lounges and enjoying the entertainment, you pay nothing more for your drinks. More importantly, for your $396, I'm going to give you $600 of my dollars to gamble with in my casino."

His widget included the room, it included the drinks, it included some extras like the champagne and souvenir dice and show tickets. It included $600 to gamble with while you were at his casino.

This widget turned that little hotel, which at the time that this started was on a Motel 6 level, into one of the largest and fastest-growing hotels on the Las Vegas Strip in its time called *Bob Stupak's Vegas World*. It eventually became *The Stratosphere*.

If you're old enough, you may recall seeing Bob's full-page ads for this widget in *Parade*, *Sports Illustrated*, *Playboy*, and in dozens and dozens of magazines and newspapers all across the country.

Bob filled his rooms by selling that widget and that was really the business that he was in, the business of selling that widget. He didn't advertise any other type of accommodations. He didn't bother advertising his hotel as a hotel. He concentrated all his efforts and all his energy and all his resources on selling that widget.

These packages were prepaid. You bought your $396 package today but you might not actually make reservations and go to the hotel until a month later, six months later, even a year later. In the interim, Bob exchanged your $396 for a certificate, a piece of paper which entitled you to all the benefits that I described. He had your

$396 in a bank account earning interest or funding construction and remodeling during that time that it was not redeemed.

If you study that example closely, you see that a fairly mundane and ordinary business, the hotel business and the hotel casino business was turned into a totally different business.

A different business was invented within the business and that new and different business became the widget that was sold to the public.

That's exactly the thinking process that you need to go through.

CREATING IRRESISTIBLE OFFERS

Bob Stupak's "widget" created an empire for him because at the time, it was irresistible and original.

With this widget, he managed to create a Godfather-level kind of offer—the kind of offer you simply cannot refuse.

Think about it—this offer, this deal, it just sounded too good to be true—room, champagne, unlimited booze, even $600 in gambling money (which had to played at the casino, it couldn't be redeemed for cash). The total package just seemed amazing.

THAT is the kind of thinking you need to put into place when creating your offers. Too many business owners come up with an offer that's practically invisible—"Save 5 percent!" or something else that involved zero imagination and barely moves the needle.

An irresistible offer (again, think "widget" because that's what you'll be promoting) bundles together a variety of elements—price, bonuses, guarantee, speed, security, etc.—into something unique and compelling. Frankly, if the widget you create doesn't cause you to pause and reflect to yourself "Am I giving away the farm here?" for at least a moment, then the offer isn't good enough.

To be truly irresistible, it should literally overwhelm the customer with value.

Now, that doesn't mean you have to take a bath on the deals you make. Quite the opposite. Stupak watched his numbers and he knew exactly what kind of ROI he got from every room key handed out. He also factored into the mix things like food, house winnings, return visits, referrals, and much more.

So the widget didn't stand alone—it was just one piece of a much larger play he had going involving his business and how he could maximize the lifetime value of every customer.

When creating your offer widgets, in the *Magnetic Marketing System* there are basically three types of offers.

→ **Lead Generation Offers**

→ **Consultation Offers**

→ **Direct Purchase or Final Offers**

Each type of offer serves a specific purpose in building a positive relationship with your prospective customer, client, or patient—establishing credibility and trust—all leading to the end goal of making the sale. Let's talk about each in a bit more detail.

LEAD GENERATION OFFERS

This is an offer whose only purpose is to, in effect, entice a prospect to raise their hand to identify and register themselves as having interest in certain subject matter, information, or goods and services, and to invite further communication with you. Often, although not always, the lead generation offer is free.

You see lead generation done by direct marketers routinely and regularly. You may not have given them much thought before, but now that you're aware of this kind of offer, you will.

For example, a national company may offer walk-in bathtubs for the elderly, advertising on cable and in national print, offering their "lead gen widget," which is a free information kit and DVD. Once someone raises their hand and requests this "kit," the company now recognizes them as "a lead" and they can follow up with focused marketing looking to make the sale.

This model is widespread across all kinds of industries, including pharmaceuticals, finance, home improvements, and many more.

Oddly enough, you rarely find a local company doing this same strategy. Instead, they immediately try to get the prospect to commit to a "free in-home estimate" or "free consultation."

This can quite often be a mistake, as it's asking too much too soon.

"Why?" you wonder… well, Arnold Taubman, one of America's most successful mall developers, coined the term "Threshold Resistance" in regards to the entrances to retail stores. I find it applies even more broadly to direct marketing.

Again, remember that your prospect doesn't want to pull out their credit card. They don't want to get off the couch. They don't want to even pick up their cell phone and punch in a number. At a mall, it's hard enough to get them to enter a retail store where God forbid they face the very real possibility of some stranger walking up and trying to sell them something.

So jumping right into "Sign up for a free consultation"—whether from a chiropractor, financial advisor, remodeler, or what-have-you is a BIG threshold to get them to cross.

That's why starting with something that has a very low barrier to entry—like "call this number and get my free report and DVD"—is much easier to convert and provides a higher response. There's less perceived risk. So those interested are more likely to respond. And by getting them to agree to that first step, albeit tiny, you increase the chances that further down the road they will become a customer, client or patient. **This is a key to magnetically attracting customers.** The addition of lead generation to your marketing system allows you to create a pool of ideal customers to directly market to.

Therefore, if your business DOES in fact require some sort of consultative-based sale (e.g., look over the home to be remodeled or assess their current financial situation), it's wise to get the ball rolling with an appropriate lead generation offer of a free report or DVD or audio.

Don't ignore this strategy if your business does NOT require a consultation. Remember, you have skepticism to overcome with almost every kind of sale, whether it's for something relatively simple like a garden shed for the backyard or a standard service like a plumber or carpenter may offer. Just about EVERY kind of business can do lead generation with this approach.

For example, if you sell garden sheds, you could offer a free DVD showing the many different ways a simple garden shed can be used to make your life more practical or fun. If you offer carpentry services, you could offer a report laying out "Seven Easy Ways to Save Serious Money When You Have to Fix Your Deck."

We call this report or DVD or whatever a Lead Generation Magnet and I'll go into more detail in an upcoming chapter.

CONSULTATION OFFERS

It's important to understand the lead generation offer as it could very well be a foreign concept to you. However, the consultation offer is probably already familiar. Indeed, it could be the basic kind of offer you're making right now in your business, especially if you're in some kind of professional service industry like dentistry, legal services, financial planning, and yes, even copywriting.

The point of a consultation offer is to compel the prospect to meet—either face to face in person or over the phone or the internet—to discuss their specific situation as it relates to your business.

Again, do not underestimate how hard it can be to get someone—who may or may not know you—to drop everything and commit to this kind of meeting. You can couch this in all kinds of friendly terms like "free" and "no obligation" and what have you, but the bottom line is, they know deep down there's going to be a sales pitch in there somewhere. They are deciding whether they want to give you an hour in their day to find out IF you are everything you say you will be. They need to trade an hour that could be spent making dinner, meeting with a new client, watching their child's soccer game, or even just the hour that they planned to spend reading a book to meet with you.

So you need to provide compelling copy that clearly explains the benefits (to them—not you), clearly articulates how easy and low-impact this meeting will be. Talking about the transformation that will take place AFTER they finish the meeting with you. Here's where my earlier points about "emotional copywriting" come into play. You're painting a picture of how their life is lacking something now, but when they finish with you, all will be right with the world.

And at the end of your meeting—or at any other point in the marketing process, it depends on your business model and how you close the deal on your goods and services—you present the offer to purchase what it is you have to sell.

DIRECT PURCHASE OR FINAL OFFER

Here's where you present the widget and ask for the sale.

The direct purchase offer you're likely most familiar with is a straight coupon offer—either from a Valpak mailing or online from Groupon or the like. Now, I'm not a champion of simply offering discounts as a strategy, but this is definitely one option.

Another common direct purchase offer, in place of or in combination with discounting, is gift with purchase where you toss in one or more bonuses.

And as we discussed earlier, when describing how to create widgets, there's other things you could integrate to make this more appealing and to drive urgency.

It's important to note that the direct purchase offer is the model used by most businesses—they go right for the sale, because they don't do any of the lead generation and—even worse—fail to follow up if the initial offer doesn't get accepted.

In the *Magnetic Marketing System*, you can go directly for the sale—and in many cases it's the right thing to do. But we don't leave that as your only option. You can, instead, work your way through the sales process with multiple steps, starting with lead generation, moving on to consultation, and then finally closing the deal with your final offer.

MEDIA

So we've got a great message, we've got a great market.

Here's the next challenge.

How do you take the message you so lovingly crafted and birthed, and deliver it via the right MEDIA to these people you've carefully selected, in a way that's effective, efficient, and affordable?

How will it magnetically attract back to you the perfect prospects who are ready, able and eager to buy, and buy only from you, so you get to sell in a competitive vacuum?

How do you do that?

It's incredibly challenging, even for business owners who are far more technologically astute than I. The laundry list of media options available changes practically with every breath you take. There's no possible way anyone could keep up.

So how do you choose?

Once you know your WHO, it's easy.

Where they live is where you target.

I know—you've been told to be EVERYWHERE for EVERYBODY. Instead, you go everywhere ONLY where your WHO is.

→ If they're on Facebook (and Facebook has amazing capabilities to segment, divide, and conquer) then you go to Facebook.

→ If they're subscribers to a highly focused, niche magazine that's eagerly awaited every month by a dedicated fan base, then you go there.

→ If they're hard-core conservatives who plan their day around talk radio, then you go there.

You do NOT go where they're NOT. It's not only unnecessary, it's a waste of time, energy, and money. You go where they ARE instead.

If you make a list, and if you stop to think about it, whatever business you're in, whatever sales career you're in, you can make a long list of media—things that you can spend money on to deliver marketing messages.

These days, everyone is infatuated with the Internet—and the systems that we teach work brilliantly online. But the Internet is not a business. It is a media, and it is not the only media.

So, while going online is one option, another option is to use traditional print advertising. This could mean direct mail, Valpak, Free Standing Inserts, Yellow Pages or displaying ads in newspapers or local periodicals.

You can go exhibit at home and consumer shows or trade shows. You can go on radio and television. You can put telemarketers on the phone. On and on and on and on.

The reality is, you should use a combination of all of the different media—in fact, a combination of online and offline.

Here's a couple things you need to know.

First of all, all that stuff works, and it all can be made to work better with good, direct response methods.

But only a handful of all those things that you can do can be converted into a system. And SYSTEM's one of my favorite words. System means reliable, consistent, and predictable results.

You get it working once and then it keeps working on its own for a long, long, long, long, long time before you have to tweak it again.

We need marketing systems.

And over the next few chapters, I'm going to lay out for you a marketing system that is so predictable, so reliable, and so consistent, that when this is working for you, you go to bed at night knowing—not hoping, wishing, or praying, but knowing—within a small, acceptable range of variance, how many good prospects, customers, clients, or patients are going to come to you by noon the next day, every single day, for as long as you use the system.

It's like a thermometer. You can turn it up or down to get more or less any time of the week, month or year that you want them. It's that scientific.

But there are some rules you must follow…

Building Business Muscle With the Ultimate Magnetic Marketing

How Fitness Business Owner Daniel Aleksa is tripling his profit and increasing retention.

Five years ago, Daniel Aleksa opened Motivators Personal Training, a 2,200 square foot boutique fitness facility.

After realizing his marketing plan of "We're open, there's the sign, people will come" wasn't working, he sought advice. Studying fitness industry marketing experts, he discovered the commonality between them: They were all students of Magnetic Marketing and Dan Kennedy.

A lot has changed for Daniel since discovering Magnetic Marketing in 2013. He married Kate, who is also his business partner, and became a parent (now with 3 kids under 3). He hired two coaches. And he's become a lot more profitable. In 2013, he was operating at about 10% profit margin. Today his profit is close to 30%. Clients pay $160 per month, and they have a lifetime value between 12 and 14 months. Here is what Daniel recommends you do to increase profits and retention and overcome other business challenges that pop up:

Hold Your Marketing Accountable

"Exposure to direct response marketing, holding your marketing accountable was one of the most valuable things I could have extracted," says Daniel. He now has a strict dedication to results. All marketing must have the potential of delivering leads or making sales. He adds, "I'm not there to get the word out, to just say hello and shake hands." For example, Daniel has found that 5Ks and ladies' night out events are great lead sources for him. His process includes evaluating the cost and objective, how many leads they receive and then figuring out how many need to convert to make it profitable.

After giving it enough time and dollars, if the marketing is not returning, they learn from it and cut it.

Test Different Marketing & Leverage What Does Best

In the beginning, Daniel was the "reluctant hero." He did all the writing and attempted to speak the language of his clients. However, recently Daniel discovered his wife is the most compelling marketing device they have. "My wife is a big piece of this gym because it's 85 percent women. They are attracted to my wife. She just had twins... and worked out almost up until term." Daniel began promoting the "Hot Mommy Makeover" at ladies' nights, putting his wife on banners and all over their marketing. He says it works better than anything he's done.

Create A Strong, Compelling, Irresistible Offer

Twenty-eight days' worth of training for $97. That's the introductory offer made

Reprinted from the NO B.S. Marketing Letter September 2015

in their Hot Mommy Makeover. Using different variations of the "under 30 days and under $100" offer has proven to be the irresistible offer that works for his business model. Daniel found "$97 is not going to scare them" and gets them in the door reliably rather than initially offering a $2,000 program.

To make his offer even more irresistible, Daniel dangles a highly desirable carrot: "Tone up in 28 days and win a salon makeover." He approaches a hair salon by offering to train their entire staff for free in exchange for the salon donating a full makeover package – hair, nails, makeup – everything. This creates extra leads, too, as the salon cross-promotes his offer to their clients.

Build Indoctrination Into Your Low-Barrier Offer

Once clients take the irresistible low-barrier offer, they enter Daniel's indoctrination phase. The goal here is to get clients to "know, like and trust Motivators Personal Training, and say to themselves, "Wow, this is a great place," says Daniel.

The indoctrination includes a minimum of five touch points within the first two weeks. New clients get a phone call after their first work-out with an offer of a couple of stretches they can do if they are feeling sore. Daniel sends a print newsletter filled with testimonials designed to sell new clients on the long-term program. He mails a "puff up card," which tells clients they are doing great. "it's puffing them up and includes two buddy passes that let them bring a friend, family, coworker for free to their next workout." Daniel also sends follow-up emails that ask how clients are feeling.

At the end of the indoctrination phase, there is a conversation to convert new clients into a long-term program ranging from eight to 16 months.

"That sort of indoctrination is certainly needed... we sell as much as 20, 30, 40 percent higher than the next guy. Without the indoctrination, they have no context or reason to understand why ours is more expensive. Our attempt is to just slug them over the head with value in their four weeks so when they see the prices at the end of it, they say, "I understand now," explains Daniel.

"I think now, more than ever, people are wanting an analog, physical experience, because everything's digital, digital, digital, and it just kind of cheapens it."

> "I think now, more than ever, people are wanting an analog, physical experience, because everything's digital, digital, digital, and it just kind of cheapens it."

Acquire Ultra-Affluent Clients

After hearing Dan Kennedy talk about the importance of acquiring clients with financial stamina, Daniel is focusing on targeting his promotions to fill classes with ultra-affluent clients who can continue on as members on long-term agreements at the highest price point. He says in 2013 he just wanted to fill the class but "now I'm focusing on the acquisition of the affluent client with financial stamina and working on how do I keep them engaged to a level that doesn't necessarily require myself personally, that is a result of our systems and putting an iron fence around them."

CHAPTER 6

The 10 Foundational Rules

I spend a good portion of my book, *The No B.S. Guide to Direct Marketing*, laying out the ironclad rules that will transform any business into an infinitely more powerful direct marketing business. These also are the foundational rules that govern *Magnetic Marketing*.

Note that these are NOT "recommendations"—consider them mandates. Gospel. Etchings in stone brought down at great peril from the mountain. Please copy them down and post them anywhere and everywhere you work so that they will remain front and center of all marketing efforts from this day forward.

Resolve now that every ad you run, every flyer you distribute, every postcard or letter you mail, every website you put up, everything and anything you do to market your business MUST adhere to these rules.

Yes, they are simplistic, dogmatic, and you will undoubtedly encounter specific situations where you find there truly is a rational reason to violate one or more.

But for now, sticking to them rigidly is the right approach, the best approach, and the approach that you can be sure of that will work. You can experiment later after you have gained practical experience in their use and have fully exorcised the demons of "brand advertising" from your mindset and your business.

RULE #1—THERE WILL ALWAYS BE AN OFFER OR OFFERS

Number one, there will always be an offer or offers. On the internet especially, there's a popular idea that content is king. I would disagree. The sale is king.

All your marketing needs to have is an offer telling your ideal prospects exactly what to do and why they want to do it right now. It should be irresistible and time sensitive and give them some kind of transformative value if they take action.

This is not just an implied offer like a store running ads, "We're here, come on in." This should **not be a common offer like, "The Sale of the Century. This Weekend Only."** Instead, ideally, yours is a Godfather's offer—an offer so big, so bold, so perfectly targeted to the WHO you've identified as your slam-dunk customer that it is impossible to refuse.

Now, this offer could be to generate a lead (with some sort of "lead generation magnet" like a free report, video, etc.) or to actually make the sale at that time. Needless to say, a great deal of thought needs to go into your offer as we explained in the previous chapter.

Regardless of the nature of the offer itself, the point is to make certain that every communication actually asks somebody to do something. Focusing on this injects a new level of discipline into all of your communications with prospects, customers, and the marketplace at large.

This rule should open your eyes to the sad reality that the vast majority of advertising presented merely shows up and talks about the marketplace, the advertiser, the wind, sun, and the rain, social values, what have you without any kind of reference to something specific to be had by immediately responding. In essence, the blimp passes by once again, fading into the sunset, leaving no trace behind. Nothing to track, nothing to measure, nothing to score. Money flies off with the wind.

When you take this kind of undisciplined approach to your marketing and simply spend and hope and guess, you're at the mercy of relying on opinion as to its effect—do you like it? Did your mother-in-law think it was humorous and expel a chuckle? Do your customers say nice things about it? Try paying your bills with that kind of feedback.

RULE #2—THERE WILL BE A REASON TO RESPOND RIGHT NOW

The hidden cost and failure in all advertising and marketing are in the "almost persuaded."

They were tempted to respond. They nearly responded. They got right up to the edge of response, but they set it aside to do it later or to mull over or to check out other options.

When they get to that edge, we must reach across and drag them past it. There must be a good reason for them not to stop short or delay or ponder, there must be urgency.

Remember, hesitation and procrastination are among the most common of human behaviors. Your prospect doesn't want to move, period. Just like Homer Simpson, the last thing he wants is put down the donut, get off the couch, and actually do something. Hence, you must provide a compelling reason to act and NOW.

There are plenty of ways to add URGENCY:

→ Tie the offer to a hard and fast deadline

→ Restrict the offer to a limited number of customers

→ Remove the bonus or gift from the deal if they don't act right away

→ Add an element of "bidding" to the deal, a la ebay

Those are just a few ideas; open your eyes to the world of experienced direct marketers out there and I'm confident you'll discover many more. Regardless, make sure to give a reason to act NOW.

RULE #3—YOU WILL GIVE CLEAR INSTRUCTIONS

Most people do a reasonably good job at following directions.

For the most part, they stop on red and go on green; stand in the lines they're told to stand in; fill out the forms they're given to fill out and applaud when the applause sign comes on.

Most people are conditioned from infancy in every environment to do as they are told. Marketers' failures and disappointments often result from giving confusing directions, or no directions at all and confused or uncertain consumers do nothing.

People rarely buy anything of consequence without being asked. You must walk your prospect through the steps you want them to take in order to make the sale.

This is far more important than you might imagine. Take to heart the old rule: "A confused buyer—WON'T buy!" Anxiety rises anytime you ask someone to do something that they're unsure of what to expect or how to carry out.

Therefore, whenever you put together any kind of marketing tool, ad, flyer, sales letter, website, phone script, etc. make sure to examine it from the perspective of an unsuspecting customer/ prospect encountering it for the very first time.

Consumers like, are reassured by, and respond to clarity. Be sure you provide it.

RULE #4—THERE WILL BE TRACKING, MEASUREMENT, AND ACCOUNTABILITY

If you want real profits from your marketing, you are no longer going to permit any advertising, marketing or selling investments to be made without directing accurate tracking, measurement and accountability.

Forget about likes, links, opens, shares, reach, visibility, views, and engagement—they can't be deposited in your bank account. All of that may be interesting, even indicative, but what matters is that for every dollar you spend, you can clearly identify how much comes back as a result.

This is for two reasons,

1. Business management by objectives is the only kind of management that actually works.

2. You need real, hard facts and data to make good, intelligent marketing decisions.

If you loop back and connect this to Rule #1, you'll find an important key in tracking—offers. Different offers can be made in different media, to different lists, and at different times. You can include and assign promotion codes to coupons, reply cards, websites, order forms, phone numbers, and so forth. With this data, you can determine which offers and variations of offers work best to which lists under what conditions.

Tough-minded management of marketing requires *knowing* things and then acting wisely upon what you know.

RULE #5—ONLY NO-COST BRAND-BUILDING

I am not opposed to brand-building.

I am opposed to paying for brand-building

Most small business owners cannot afford to properly invest in brand-building. I do not believe it is a wise investment for small business owners and entrepreneurs, nor do I believe it is even necessary. You can acquire all the brand power you need as a no-cost byproduct of profitable direct response advertising and marketing as described in this book.

My preferred strategy is simple: buy response, gratefully accept brand-building as a bonus. NEVER buy brand-building and hope for response as a bonus, unless you simply want to spend Daddy's fortune out of spite.

Paying for traditional brand-building may be fine, even essential for giant companies with giant budgets engaged in a fierce combat over shelf space and consumer recognition. So if you're Coors or Heinz or some other company like that, feel free to play with the shareholders' money to buy name recognition. But if you're an entrepreneur playing with your own marbles, beware, because copying what the big companies do to build their brands can bankrupt you.

Even though held in high regard by media companies and advertising agencies alike, "brand" is not the holy grail magically able to cure all your business woes. Brand-building is best left to very patient marketers with very deep pockets filled with other people's money. You are far better served by focusing on leads, customers, sales, and profits directly driven by your marketing system.

RULE #6—THERE WILL BE FOLLOW UP

People read your ad, get your letter, see your sign, find you online, etc.

They call or visit your website or place of business.

They ask your receptionist or staff questions.

And sadly, in far too many cases, that's it.

There's not even the slightest attempt to capture the prospect's name, physical address, or email address. There's no offer to immediately send an information package, free report, or coupons.

This is criminal waste. I've been poor and I abhor and detest and condemn waste.

When you fail to follow up, you are simply shrugging your shoulders and accepting waste as yet another cost of doing business. This is madness.

When you invest in advertising and marketing, you're not just paying for the customers you get. You are paying for each lead you generate, every call, every walk-in, every email, every reaction and response of any kind.

If an ad costs you $1000 and you get fifty calls, every call you fail to follow up on is exactly like pulling a $20 bill from your wallet, taking a match to it, and watching it go up in flames. So unless you truly do have money to burn, you need to make sure to follow up with every lead that comes through your door.

There are hundreds of variations for follow up campaigns and strategies, blending offline with online. Here are just few ways you can follow up:

1. **Restate, ReSell, and Extend the Same Offer**—present what they didn't do or buy again in the best way possible. You can do this in a straightforward manner with letters or emails. You can also use "retargeting" online technology to keep the offer in front of someone long after they've seen it the first time—they'll see it on other websites they visit, their Facebook feed, and so on.

2. **Provide a Stern or Humorous "Second Notice" Tied to an Onrushing Deadline**—present the offer again, reemphasizing the approaching deadline.

3. **"Third and Final Notice"**—Tie this communication to the deadline and the disappearance of the offer.

4. **Change the Offer**—Sometimes you can change the offer relatively easily, by offering new or extended installment payment terms, by swapping out a bonus for something different, etc.

Doing nothing with even one lead is like flushing money down the toilet. It is a serious lapse in judgment and waste of precious resources every time you fail to follow-up with every lead or every customer.

RULE #7—THERE WILL BE STRONG COPY

The fact is, there is enormous, ever-growing, almost overwhelming competition for attention and interest—a daily tsunami of clutter that must be cut through or circumvented. In this environment, where literally tens of thousands of messages bombard your prospects every day, the ordinary and the normal are ignored, the cautious and calm messages unnoticed.

You can't send a shy, timid Casper Milktoast to knock on a door of a home or walk into a business and beg in barely a whisper for a few moments of the prospect's time. So you can't do that with a postcard, letter, flyer, newsletter, email, web video, etc. either.

You want to send the Incredible Hulk instead—huge, glowing neon green, stomping, impossible to ignore. He shows up and the guy drops whatever he's been doing, and pays attention.

But the copy can't just shout. Loud but irrelevant isn't much better than quiet yet relevant. Loudness can grab attention, but you can't convert it to interest. The Incredible Hulk stomping into your office would get your attention, but he'd still have trouble bridging to interest and having you engage in a conversation with about just any new product.

Strong copy can be sensational and attention-commanding, but does so in a way that establishes relevance and credible authority—creating proactive interest in our information, goods, and services.

Here's a good example of a strong headline making a real benefit-oriented promise:

Find Out Why Seven Out of Ten Homes Don't Sell
Special report reveals the four most common mistakes that can cost you thousands

Most strong copy gets written backwards, starting from the customer's interests, desires, frustrations, fears, thoughts, feelings, and experiences (remember the emphasis earlier on nailing down the WHO?)—and then journeys forward to reveal a solution tied to your business.

Most ineffective copy takes the reverse path: starting instead with the company, product or service and its features, benefits, comparative superiority, and price. This is the common default approach the overwhelming majority of advertisers, copywriters, and salespeople fall back to, rather than developing a more creative, customer-focused approach.

Here are two major mistakes your copy can't afford to make:

1. **Writing factually and "professionally" rather than emotionally**. Great copy communicates conversationally, one-on-one, just like you would sitting across the table from a friend you can't wait to let in on something wonderful you've just discovered. And it makes no difference whether you're selling to Fortune 1000 CEOs or Al Bundy in his trailer—your best approach is to write like you talk, speaking passionately from the heart with deeply emotional appeals.

2. **Being timid or bland in your claims and promises.** Many believe their customers, clients, or patients are smarter and more sophisticated than others, at least immune to sensationalism and hyperbole, perhaps offended by it, and they discredit themselves by engaging in it. Wrong. These beliefs are in contradiction to facts and experience, for in every category of product or service, in media directed at presumably educated, sophisticated people, I can find examples of ads making grandiose and extraordinary claims that succeed mightily. Zig Ziglar was right: "Timid salesmen have skinny kids"—no matter who they're selling to.

The fact you must embrace about strong sales copy is that you need it and you may have to learn to write it for yourself. If this concept happens to be brand new to you, start with my **Magnetic Marketing System and Toolkit** available at www.MagneticMarketing.com or consider the option of having our team write this for you.

RULE #8—IT WILL LOOK LIKE MAIL-ORDER ADVERTISING

This rule is a great simplifier, because it ends your paying attention to—and trying to emulate—the overwhelming majority of all the advertising you see on TV, in magazines, in newspapers, online; by your peers and competitors. You are to go blind to anything except *pure* mail-order advertising. Anything else, shut the door, ignore.

I am specifically speaking of their formats, layout, and appearance of advertising—whether print ad or a webpage or any other item.

Here's exactly the type of ad I'm talking about:

Classic mail-order ads are typically broken up into one quarter, one-half, and one quarter of the page, give or take. The top quarter is for headline and subheads; the middle half for presentation of product or proposition, sometimes aided by testimonials; the bottom quarter for the offer and clear response instructions, often with a coupon.

The most frequently used alternative is the advertorial, which mimics an article.

The other reliable format is that of a letter, from you to the reader, at whatever length is necessary to do the job. I have clients mailing 4, 8, 16, 24 and in one case, 64-page sales letters. One of these, a 16-page one, literally tacked up online as a website, having traffic driven to it, has produced $1 million a year for nine years running.

To see real mail-order advertising, you need to assemble a diverse assortment of magazines in which highly successful mail-order companies consistently run full-page advertisements. These include *Reader's Digest Large Print Edition*, tabloids like the *National Enquirer*, and business publications like *Investors Business Daily* and *Entrepreneur*. Also check out special interest magazines for model railroad hobbyists, gun enthusiasts, horse lovers, etc. as you'll find fractional and full-page mail-order ads.

Tear out and keep these ads as research; *discard all others*. Let these ads be your only models. If you respond to some, your mailbox will soon be full of direct mail that also follows classic formats and architecture.

You'll eventually have a collection of advertisements that—if studied and modeled for your own use—represents money in the bank.

If you're looking for a shortcut, I have compiled a few along the way, with templates in my *Magnetic Marketing System and Toolkit* (available at www.MagneticMarketing.com.)

RULE #9—RESULTS RULE. PERIOD.

Results rule. Period.

Do not let anyone confuse, bamboozle or convince you that anything else is of any importance. Nobody's opinion counts—even yours.

And there's no excuse for not assessing results any more. With today's technology, it's easier than ever to link and track specific promotions to quantifiable results. You can even do what's called "split-testing" or "A-B" testing, where you match one headline against another to see which produces the best results, and then continue the process over and again. Test. Monitor. Adjust. The goal is to gradually achieve the very best results possible.

The only thing that matters is the answer to the question, "What results did I get?" When you implement this into your marketing approach and marketing messages, you change the way you communicate with your prospects and customers dramatically and forever.

> **NOTE:** A lot of what you have just read in the previous rules may seem weird, sound funny, or feel wrong to you. Too bold. Too aggressive. Too hype-y. Too unprofessional. Too far outside the box of what's deemed "correct" for your profession or field. That's understandable. But it doesn't matter because remember, <u>your opinions NEVER COUNT.</u> You don't get a vote, neither does your wife, your mother, your golfing buddy, neighbor, competitor, employee, nobody gets a vote. The only vote that counts is the customer's and the only legal, valid ballots are cash, checks, and credit cards.

RULE #10—YOU WILL BE A TOUGH-MINDED DISCIPLINARIAN AND PUT YOUR BUSINESS ON A STRICT DIRECT MARKETING DIET

Many business owners who perennially struggle and suffer are very much aware of things that need doing but simply lack the will to do them.

Maybe it's a longtime vendor or employee or client, now a "friend," who you know is toxic and needs to be replaced, but you can't muster the will to fire them.

Maybe there's an ad that you keep spending money on that you know is failing to deliver results, but you lack the will to fix it or shut it down.

Maybe there's a website you know isn't producing either, but the very thought of getting it remade is painful, so it stays as is.

From this point forward, with ALL advertising and marketing, you have to be thick-skinned about criticism, tough-minded about money invested, extremely disciplined in thought and action, and dedicated to carrying out your game plan, all fueled by a resolute will to win.

IMPORTANT:

Anything that doesn't conform to the 10 Rules discussed in this chapter, do not let in at all. Just say no. And bar the door.

When you DO implement all these into your marketing approach and marketing messages, you change—for the better—the way you communicate with your prospects and customers dramatically and forever.

Peterman Heating, Cooling & Plumbing

Building a Better Fence

How Peterman Heating, Cooling & Plumbing Doubled Their Business (And You Can Too) Using Retention, Ascension And Referral Strategies

Three years ago, the Peterman's set an aggressive goal: grow their business 100% in three years. They are on target to exceed that goal.

Founded in 1986 out of his garage by Pete Peterman, Peterman Heating Cooling and Plumbing grew to 20 employees. His sons, Chad and Tyler, joined him in the business eight years ago and began looking for ways to grow the company even more.

After being referred by a fellow entrepreneur, the Petermans became Magnetic Marketing Members. Since then they've grown to 80 employees and three locations (Indianapolis, Columbus, and Lafayette, Indiana). They've significantly increased the lifetime value of their customers and created an iron fence around them. Loyalty, customer retention, and referrals have skyrocketed.

Speaking with Chad Peterman left me wishing they'd open a location in my town. Read on for some great ideas about how to increase your retention, build ascension and get more and better referrals.

Four Questions That Build A Better Fence

Sending a print newsletter every single month was a first step to putting a fence around the Peterman's herd. However, the Petermans were still experiencing problems with annual retention. People weren't renewing their service contracts. They looked at other industries outside of their own to see how people were being successful. A new Peak Performer member, Chad Peterman turned to the Magnetic Marketing community for solutions. "For me personally, that's been one of the big things I've challenged myself with is utilizing the community more and understanding how many great people are out there." Here are the questions and answers that helped shape the Peterman's improved plan:

1) What can you re-frame to create more value?

"What's common in our industry is a service contract," Chad explained. "And that's usually what it's called. We come out and we'll service your furnace, your air conditioner and so on when it's time."

The Petermans discovered they weren't placing enough importance with their employees out in the field to sell these service contracts. Plus, a service contract doesn't sound too sexy either.

The Petermans renamed the service contract, calling it the Peterman Protection Club. "We said we're not call-

Reprinted from the NO B.S. Marketing Letter August 2018

ing it a contract," Chad said. "No one wants to sign a contract. What we're going to call it is a membership." Now instead of paying an annual fee, club members are on a monthly auto-pay system.

The new membership plan has been huge for the Petermans. In the first five months of 2018 alone, they've signed up 1500 new members. Plus, with the autopay, they no longer worry about renewing customers.

2) What exclusive perks and benefits can you offer?

Under a standard service contract, normally the customer is charged a reduced fee. The Petermans decided to do away with that. "For all our members, we don't charge a service fee as long as you're paying your membership monthly," Chad said. Among the perks, members have a special members-only hotline phone number they can call 24 hours a day and get immediate service. They receive special discounts with additional discounts for teachers, first responders, veterans, and seniors. They even created a special guarantee for members.

"One of the guarantees we give our members is what we call our owner's voice guarantee," Chad said. "Basically, what that says is if you have service from us and you feel like something didn't go right ... you were wronged ... a situation wasn't handled properly, you can call up and talk to one of us (the owners) and we're going to make it right for you."

Building on that, the Petermans put themselves front and center showcasing they are a family-owned business, a key differentiator from their competitors. "We're not hiding behind any sort of brand name," Chad explained. Putting their picture on every piece of marketing and their voice on every radio ad has eased customer's fears about being overcharged or charged for something they don't need and so on. "I've talked to many customers and it works both ways," Chad said. "It works for trust for them and it also works for us too, because I want to know if something's going wrong. Did we screw up? If we did, let's get it fixed."

Chad believes this has been good for retention too. "It was amazing that once we started building that kind of brand, the people started to latch on. People started to say, "Oh, you're those guys ... No one else in the city really does that," Chad continued, "They know who they're dealing with. It's not just some company with a bunch of shareholders and all they really care about is the profit margin."

3) How can we create peer influence, recognition, and status?

Building their club, they added items for ascension. "We've got three levels of membership so customers can move up if they want more services or they get a different piece of equipment or whatever."

Another element of the Peterman Protection Club is charity. The Petermans have a list of four charities for members to choose from when they become a member. "When we make a repair at your home, we donate $5 in your name to that particular charity," Chad said. "This has been a huge selling point for our members."

4) How can we offer more or a better

service option?

The Petermans expanded beyond heating and cooling services to "maximize the home." Services added include plumbing, drain, and excavation and they are adding home performance. "A big point when it comes to retention and ascension is the ability to offer a customer who has already placed their trust in you ... more services that are related to your current service."

An Internal Referral System That Drives Growth And Retention

The Petermans have a system in place for getting online reviews which helps get them in the top of local listings when people do a Google search. Technicians in the field are instructed to bring up reviews at both the beginning and end of the service call. At the beginning they say, "It's our goal today to provide five-star service. If at any time I should fall below five stars, please let me know so I can get it corrected." At the end they say, "Hey, Mr. /Mrs. Smith, did you receive five-star service today?" When the customer says yes, the technician responds, "Well that's great. If you would, we'd really like you to share your thoughts about that online so that other customers like yourself can receive that same five-star service."

What Chad is most proud of is their internal referral system that is driving growth in more ways than one.

"People are ultimately what's going to drive our business and drive our growth," Chad said, "We put in an in-

ternal referral program that pays any employee $100 if they refer someone to work here that's qualified and we interview."

The referred person doesn't have to be hired for the employee to receive the referral fee. "If that employee they referred is hired on, after 90 days the referring employee gets $150 a month, every month, for up to five years," Chad explained. "And so long as the referring and the referral are still employed here."

Half of their new hires come from their internal referral system.

The Petermans also applied retention strategies internally. "These marketing principles can be applied to creating a culture within your business and understanding that you're not only marketing to your outside customer, especially in industries like ours ... service-based person-to-person," Chad said. "It's key in employee retention. When you talk about trades, there aren't as many people out there. It's kind of drying up. So, if you find a good one, you better keep them, and you better keep them happy."

The Petermans dug deep to create a culture that makes their employees feel appreciated and valued. The goal: To be the best place anyone that works there has ever worked. "It was just creating a place where people want to come to work and want to be good at what they do," Chad said. "I think a lot of people would be amazed that when you create a place like that, you differentiate yourself from all others. That shows through when the guy you send out to someone's home really believes he works for somewhere special and that they care about him. He wants to

Reprinted from the NO B.S. Marketing Letter August 2018

be successful because he knows that will make the company successful. That shows through to the customer and they begin to trust you a whole heck of a lot more."

"In any business, the people are what's going to make it. When you can find really, really good people you can soar to heights that you never thought imaginable."

"As we have really ingrained that philosophy, our company has grown exponentially," Chad said. "Customers seem to talk about how our employees care more and more as we continue to improve our culture within."

Not everything the Petermans have done has been successful. Chad admits they've fallen short and made mistakes. However, the Peterman's commitment to creating retention, an ascension ladder, and a referral system has paid off big-time. Besides the growth and revenue, they've found their employees and customers are more loyal. Customers spend more money with them (and less with competitors), are less sensitive about price and give more referrals. And one final piece of advice: reach out and utilize the Magnetic Marketing Community like the Petermans to create shortcuts to success.

BUILDING YOUR MAGNETIC MARKETING SYSTEM

CHAPTER 7

Your Magnetic Attraction System

What I'm going to describe to you over the next three chapters represents the foundational components of the complete *Magnetic Marketing System*. In over four decades, I've never met a single person who couldn't take this foundation and apply it for use in their business.

When you put this system in place, you'll have a repeatable, reliable machine working for you 24/7/365 to attract-convert-retain customers. No more guesswork. No more "feast or famine." No more random acts of marketing.

In this chapter, we'll cover your **Magnetic Attraction System**— built to attract prospects who you know fit your targeted WHO and allowing them to raise their hand indicating that they have a problem you can solve thanks to what you have to offer, be it product, service, or some mix of both.

The diagram below shows how the Attraction System works:

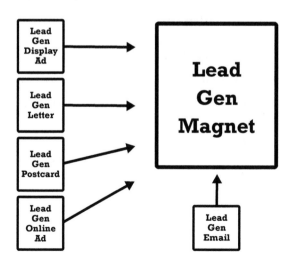

The Attraction System uses a variety of MEDIA channels where your target prospects hang out to let them know about your Lead Generation Magnet.

These can include magazine ads, banner ads on websites, Pay-Per-Click ads, emails sent to lists they've subscribed to, direct mail, business cards you hand out when meeting someone, display ads in newspapers, ValPak coupons, and so on.

The Lead Generation Magnet is the special "Widget" you are offering to get individuals—from the greater population of prospects—to indicate interest and thereby transform themselves from a prospect into a "LEAD."

Once a lead raises their hand, you now have permission (and the responsibility) to follow up with them regarding the information they requested. For example:

→ **If they asked about ideas for staging and selling their house, you can follow up with them on this.**

→ **If they asked about ensuring their children are protected in an estate plan, you can follow up with them on this.**

→ **If they asked about learning how to hit the golf ball ten yards farther without new clubs, you can follow up with them on this.**

Everyone who raises their hand gets put into a "bucket" or database or list from which you then follow up with messaging aimed at converting them from a lead to a paying customer.

This approach transforms your advertising from a "hope but can't tell if it works" model to a "know if it works" system. Now you're investing in reaching out directly to people you KNOW you can help and who have indicated they have a problem you can solve. You can run the numbers based on the results you're getting from your lead generation ads—calculate to see that for every $1 you invest you get $2-$4 or more back. This is a huge improvement over Goodyear blimp advertising where there's no way to accurately measure and you have no idea whether the ads have any effect at all.

CREATING YOUR LEAD GENERATION REPORT / GUIDE / MAGNET

Typically, your Lead Generation Magnet is information that has real value to the prospect.

It can be simple, brief, delivered via offline or online media, and crafted to attract exactly the prospect, customer, client, or patient you want.

It can be a free report, or a checklist, or even a cheat sheet on a subject of prime interest to your preferred customer.

The purpose for all of these is to position you and your company as reliable, knowledgeable, experts in your field.

Your Lead Generation Magnet has four main jobs:

1.   First, to generate and enhance response to advertising.

2.   Second, to reinforce and strengthen the prospect's unhappiness with the current circumstances and problems he has that you can provide the solution to.

3.   Third, to establish both your expertise and empathy.

4.   Fourth, positioning so that the prospect is predisposed to accept your recommendations favorably.

In many cases, the free report is nothing more or less than a disguised, persuasive long copy sales letter, but if you called it that, no one would want it.

Instead, it's best to include legitimately valuable information. When you include such information, the prospect will see that you are a good source for answers to his problems, needs, and desires.

A lot of people balk at giving away valuable information, but that's a huge mistake. You give to get. If you don't reveal anything of value in your Lead Generation Magnet, the prospect can assume there's no value in your products or services either.

Here are some examples of information-based Lead Generation Magnets.

If I were a chiropractor my report might be, "*Six Ways to Have a Pain-Free Back in Six Weeks*." Obviously one of the six ways would involve coming into my office for an exam, and possibly treatment. The other five ways would be useful things the person can do on their own to relieve pain.

If I were in real estate, my report might be, "*Fourteen Little Known Ways to Get Top Dollar for Your Home, Even in a Tight Market*." One of those ways would be to list the home with me, and in that section of the report I'd thoroughly describe all the benefits of listing with me. The other thirteen ways would be information about inexpensively cleaning up the house and yard, staging a house, writing Craigslist ads, and so on. Through these thirteen ways, I'd show off my expertise and know-how, and convey the difficulty of doing everything without me.

If I were in multi-level marketing, my report might be titled, "*Ten Best Ways to Create a Half-Million-Dollar Retirement Nest Egg, Even if Starting Late, Even with Little or No Money to Invest.*" The report could include information on buying real estate with no money down, on tax-sheltered savings vehicles like IRAs, on mutual funds. One of the ten ways would be developing a network marketing business in your spare time.

Here are a few important writing tips.

Avoid "me, me, me, we, we, we" speak.

Some Lead Generation Magnets talk too much about the company and not enough about the prospect. He does not care about you, or your company per se, he only cares about the wonderful things that will happen to him as a result of doing business with your company. Translate every fact and feature listed in your report into a benefit. Be you-oriented, not me-oriented. Use all the data you gathered about your who, and talk to them in their language and about their real problems.

Don't overeducate.

You want to inform and impress, but not tell everything you know. Tell people what to do, but not how to do it. Let them take the next step to get the exact how-tos. (In fact, one of the best responses you can get from your Lead Generation Magnet is "can you help me do this?")

Don't forget the call to action.

If you don't have a call to action (CTA), you've wasted your time and money. To paraphrase Zig Ziglar, "Is your free report a sales professional, or a professional visitor?"

Tell the prospect exactly what to do, when, why, and what will happen once he does. It's helpful to offer an immediate gratification incentive for that requested action, such as a special bonus, or a discount. The CTA could be a number of things, depending on how complex your sales funnel needs to be.

→ You could go directly for the sale of a product or service, including pricing, features, bonuses, guarantee, even a deadline.

→ You could instead offer some type of consultation, with an invitation to set up an in-person call or face-to-face meeting.

→ Or you could send them to a website or some other additional information resource.

Create and use powerful titles.

The title of your Lead Generation Magnet is very important. Like a headline, it has to interest people enough to want it, and then motivate them to consume it when they get it.

Take the time to create a really powerful title. Where do you get great titles? Model the attention-getting headlines you can find on supermarket tabloids, like *The Enquirer*, and on the covers of magazines like *Cosmopolitan*, *Readers Digest*, and others.

These headlines have to sell those magazines off the rack. Of course, the subject matter probably won't fit your business, but the structures of these headlines will.

Making the Lead Generation offer.

Making the offer for the Lead Generation Magnet involves two steps:

➔ **Step 1: Sell the prospect on getting the Lead Generation Magnet.**

➔ **Step 2: Collect contact information for use in follow up.**

(After you finish Step 2, you deliver the Lead Generation Magnet, which leads right into the Conversion System, which I'll discuss in the next chapter.)

Let's talk about Step 1, which involves making a strong sales pitch to convince them to request the Lead Generation Magnet.

Do NOT underestimate the difficulty in doing this, even though it's probably something you'll be giving away for FREE. People remain reluctant to share contact information, especially given the amount of unwanted SPAM they suspect will come their way, as well as privacy concerns.

So you need to very clearly make the case why your Lead Generation Magnet will solve a specific problem, heal a burning pain point, or address a real heart-felt concern they're dealing with.

Your options for your Lead Generation Magnet are many and varied:

➔ Business card

➔ Postcard

➔ Phone script

➔ Website

➔ Facebook/YouTube/Social Media

➔ Banner ad

➔ Valpak insert

➔ TV or Radio commercial

➔ Email

➔ Speaking

You can (and should) offer your Lead Generation Magnet anywhere and everywhere.

If you do so in person, it's easy—just get the prospect's business card or contact info. Then send them the Lead Generation Magnet. Over the phone, just write it down. You can also drive people to an 800 number with a recorded message and have them leave their info there. While this may sound old school, it remains quite effective, especially when dealing with target markets that skew older.

A client of mine with one of the most productive lead generation ad campaigns on radio nationwide instructs listeners to call a voicemail number and leave their email address. Then he'll send them his free report, which has a sexy, exciting title, and promise of interest to his target market.

Don't miss that point—your Lead Generation Magnet needs to sound sexy, exciting, informative—the magic pill to cure whatever ails you. The ad copy used to promote it likewise has to frame its benefits and value with powerful, emotional language. The Lead Generation Magnet offers transformation, pure and simple, and anyone would be a fool not to take advantage of it and now.

One of the primary mechanisms today for collecting contact

information is online with a dedicated, simple webpage called a landing page or squeeze page.

You probably already have a big, fat, catchall site that has a mountain of content on it.

If you're going to do lead generation, you should not send prospects into that. Instead, send them to a very simple landing page that works just like a clerk answering the phone.

The landing page or squeeze page is very, very simple. This is where you're going to capture the person's contact information who has come to your website from one of your lead generation pieces.

The website is simple because the only reason they're coming to it is to give you their contact information in exchange for your Lead Generation Magnet, so that's all you want to show them. It doesn't include any kind of navigation options or a menu bar with "Home," "About," etc. so they can't get lost someplace else on your website. The only purpose of this page is to collect contact information so you can send them your Lead Generation Magnet, and then follow up.

You're not trying to build a brand. Not trying to entertain or inform. You're not trying to get likes, or anything like that—although those are not inherently bad. What you are trying to do, and what you want to measure, is to get the people who do show up to give you their contact information. That is the one and only goal of your landing page.

Once you have their information, you send them your Lead Generation Magnet and then put them into your Magnetic Conversion System.

IT'S ALL ABOUT MAGNETIC ATTRACTION

This chapter should make 100 percent clear what I mean by Magnetically Attracting leads as opposed to chasing them.

Yes, you lay out the offer of a Lead Generation Magnet—the

free report, the information kit, DVD, audio, checklist, etc.—to everyone in your WHO that you can. But it's not chasing, it's simply laying it out there to see if anyone's interested enough to step out of the pack and raise their hand.

By doing so, you've enticed them to take that very first step on their own. They've crossed the first threshold barrier. It's a tiny step to be sure, but it's an important one. They've said YES for the first time about something you have to offer.

Now it's up to you to build upon that momentum in your Magnetic Conversion System.

Gene Fetty

Transcending Commodity and Defying Comparison

How Gene Fetty Is Using Authority to Break His Dent Repair Business Away From the Pack

Making your business into a "category of one" creates huge advantages. Price comparison disappears. Word of mouth advertising is significant. And your business may attract free advertising through media attention.

Gene Fetty, the owner of Dent Repair Now (dentrepairnow.com), a paintless dent repair (PDR) service which fixes minor dents and dings without having to paint your car or motorcycle, has been in business going on 16 years. A quick internet search revealed 30 competitors in Pittsburgh and the surrounding tri-state area where Gene provides service to both car dealers and body shops on the wholesale side and individuals on the retail side.

Despite years of experience, Gene's business took a hit when algorithm changes by Google landed him with a lot more competition. "I thought we were diversified and doing everything well," Gene said. "Until Google started making changes to how they served the search results in our local area."

Looking for answers, Gene tuned into a copywriting podcast where he heard David Garfinkel mention Magnetic Marketing. When Gene looked into the company, he discovered that it was the same Dan Kennedy he had read 20 years earlier. (Gene originally read Dan's book, The Ultimate Sales Letter. Not understanding the concepts, he placed the book on a bookshelf.) After rediscovering Dan, Gene bought another book by Dan, *No B.S. Direct Marketing: The Ultimate No Holds Barred Kick Butt Take No Prisoners Direct Marketing for Non-Direct Marketing Businesses*. "I read the whole book on a road trip for vacation last summer," Gene said. "It piqued my interest and I signed up this past fall with Magnetic Marketing."

Gene dug in. Since becoming a member in late 2017, he's completed and implemented principles from Magnetic Marketing, attended a Fast Implementation Boot Camp, and joined his local Magnetic Marketing chapter led by Becky Auer.

These actions have spurred several "lightbulb moments" for Gene, causing him to do a complete overhaul of the way he markets his business, including targeting new markets, completely redoing his website and all of his marketing to incorporate direct response principles.

One of his biggest discoveries has been authority. Because while Gene had created authority in his market, he wasn't leveraging it. Gene does a podcast, "PDR Marketing Minute," which rides on the tail of the biggest podcast in the PDR industry. He's a paid speaker and does advanced training inside the world's largest online training com-

Reprinted from the NO B.S. Marketing Letter June 2018

pany for PDR. He's even developed dent repair techniques and a course called The PDR Video Course that trains other PDR specialists.

While attending a Fast Implementation Boot Camp in December 2017, Gene connected with his local chapter Certified Magnetic Marketing Advisor (CMMA), Becky Auer. It was this conversation that helped him realize he should leverage his authority. "When I was talking to Becky in Atlanta about my background with the podcast and being a paid speaker ... seeing the look on her face when I explained the expert position I had inside my industry," Gene said, "I thought, 'Wow, maybe I need to pay a little bit more attention to my status inside of my industry and that can help build my business.'"

Building the Gene Fetty Brand

Excited about what he had discovered, Gene gave his company a complete makeover, converting everything to direct- response and putting his authority front and center. Although at first, he says he wasn't exactly sure how to roll his expert status into his business. Digging into Dan Kennedy principles, going to local chapter meetings and enlisting the help of his chapter leader provided answers. "The new website, it's all branded," Gene explained, "There is nobody else around that is major and has this status in this whole market. The category of one is the whole approach we're taking."

Here's what Gene did to leverage his authority in his new website, he ...

Highlights his expert status. Gene uses photos of himself at speaking engagements demonstrating he's more than just a technician.

"We're still five stars across the board on all review platforms…we use that to close sales."

Showcases himself as an inventor. Gene lets people know he is the one people inside the industry come to for training on techniques. "There's one particular dent, we call it a jeep dent," Gene explains, "When you're taking your doors off your Jeep Wrangler if you're not careful, they put a very distinct dent on one spot of the car. I literally came up with the process to repair those 100 percent of the time."

- "I've literally had people call and say I need you to come and fix my car ... I don't care what it costs. I've seen your videos."

- Personalizes his business. Gene has professional headshots he includes on his website. He also puts his picture on his warranty cards, guarantee cards, business cards and referral cards he gives out. "The power of personalizing your business instead of being a Coca Cola or a McDonalds where it is all branding and brand recognition and costs millions of dollars. None of us have that kind of a budget to do that. The face of your company is enormous." Putting his face out there is paying off. For example, Gene did Facebook Live events announcing the opening of his new shop. Gene says, "People come in and say, 'I saw you on Facebook, can you come look at my car?' "

- Offers lead magnets demonstrating expertise. "We're creating guides and checklists," Gene said, "A free checklist to see if your dent is a good candidate for paintless dent repair, for example."

In addition to leveraging his authority, Gene is using other Magnetic Marketing methods to put his company even further ahead of the pack. Here are some top takeaways making a difference for Gene:

- Find where your potential prospects are hanging out: During a mastermind meeting, Gene was challenged with coming up with advertising where damage to automobiles happens. "Shopping centers were one of the places," Gene said. "Long story short, an opportunity to place an ad on shopping carts was perfect." Gene confessed his first attempt was a vanilla, branding type ad though. When he got no response, Gene said that was THE spark that drove him to start using the direct response methods Dan Kennedy talked about in his book.

- Segment-specific target audiences with microsites: "We are the only company in Pittsburgh that specializes in and has the proper tooling to do motorcycle repairs," Gene said. "So, we're building a microsite specifically for motorcycle repairs."

- Identify invisible prospects. "Our biggest problem forever is that 99% of our customers never knew the process we do even existed," Gene said. "It's just not a well-known service. The prospects that are out there are reaching out to their insurance company." (Gene will also be doing a microsite targeting insurance agents, something no one else in his industry is doing.)

- Include language specific to your target. "A great tip I picked up was to go and interview insurance agents to use their terminology when targeting them."

- Pay it forward. "We reached out to a local technician and did a Facebook Live after a hail storm," Gene said. During the event, Gene went over a report he created called, The Five Dirty Secrets Your Insurance Company Doesn't Want You To Know About Hail Repair. Then he did a Q & A. "It was all very expert-driven, instead of brand-driven or giving money away to get people in," Gene said. The 30-minute event closed $3000.00 in business.

Monetizing His Expert Status

While Gene was getting paid to speak to and train others in his industry, he says he became really excited when he realized he could also use his authority to create additional revenue streams.

Using what he learned about copywriting at the Fast Implementation Boot Camp, Gene went back and wrote a long-form email to send to his list of PDR business owners. "It went to my small list of 300 people in the industry… following the roadmap for creating an offer," Gene said. "I put it out there and did just shy of $8000.00 on my first email."

Another lightbulb moment followed—one that Gene says he is REALLY excited about. "I've got a handful of companies across the country that I'm

Reprinted from the NO B.S. Marketing Letter June 2018

working with to implement a full direct response approach," Gene said. "My thought was, I'm going to implement all of this for Dent Repair Now anyway, why don't I use my expert status, bring some other companies in, and get paid to implement it. When I'm done, the idea is to have a turnkey business-in-a-box plan that I can turn around and sell or license to the industry." (At the time of writing, Gene was scheduled to launch this in May 2018.)

"My lifestyle change, for now, is big change and big work," Gene said. "But part of what attracted me to Magnetic Marketing is the lifestyle liberation." Gene sees that on the horizon and is doing the work now to get his business running on autopilot, so he can spend more time with his wife, Melissa, daughter Elena and son Mack taking more vacations, boating, fishing, and hunting.

CHAPTER 8

Your Magnetic Conversion System

Now that you have gotten your prospect to raise their hand, it's time to fire up your **Magnetic Conversion System**—the goal of which is to turn them from someone who is merely interested into a paying customer.

The diagram below shows the different elements of the Conversion System:

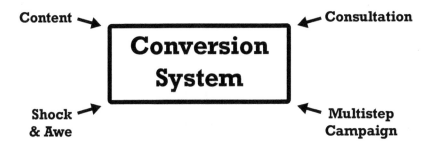

It's important to note that it's up to YOU to define exactly how configure this system. The different components, each of which I'll describe on the following pages, can be mixed and matched and sequenced in different ways.

The key, however, is to implement SOMETHING. Far too many businesses totally drop the ball when it comes to following up with leads who have already made it clear, either through action or communication, that they're interested in what you have to offer. It boggles the mind—you've paid good money for inventory, rent, power, licensing, website hosting, advertising and more, yet you're willing to watch all that go down the drain by failing to follow up.

Indeed, this should inspire you because by putting this Conversion System in place in your business, you will literally create an unfair advantage over your competition, who almost certainly won't do anything anywhere close to, or as detailed, or as systematic.

All the components of the system are based on one overriding principle:

"Show Up Like No One Else."

For just a second, let's go back to that question I said you should ask yourself when creating your Unique Selling Proposition (USP). Do you recall? It goes like this:

"Why should I choose to do business with you versus any and every other option available to me in your category?"

This is such a powerful question and you HAVE to be able to answer it in every communication you make with future and even current clients. Because as they say, every horse eventually goes lame—you can't simply assume that just because you've convinced someone to buy from you once they'll continue along that path forever. You constantly have to provide a good answer to that question throughout the entire customer life cycle.

Therefore, your goal in your Conversion System, is to show up like nobody else. Stick out like a sore thumb among the tens of thousands of sales messages bombarding your prospects every day. And when you show up at the door—standing out from the semi-washed competitive masses—you arrive not only looking like something truly special, but you bring heightened value that's clearly different.

It's important to understand that the higher up the income ladder you go, people will pay more for WHO you are rather than WHAT you do. The WHAT of what you do can easily be turned into a commodity. But WHO you are is unique—there's only one, and therefore the value is established accordingly.

Showing up like no one else reinforces that fact, which is why it must stay top of mind through all your communications as a Magnetic Marketer.

Let's talk about a few ways to do just that.

MULTISTEP CAMPAIGN

Most people's marketing is not very sophisticated at all. Here's what it looks like. Print up a brochure. A lot of them. Put them in a burlap sack. Rent a plane. Fly low. Shake sack. Hope.

We can do better.

What we want to do is identify a small, carefully selected, manageable target market and set out to become the dominant presence in that target market in as short a period of time as possible.

Why small? The biggest marketing mistake most businesses make is marketing too big. I'll ask, "What's your target market?" "Detroit." "Well, if we send one postcard to every adult who lives in the greater Detroit area once a year, which can hardly be called an intensive campaign, what's our budget got to be?" The guy says, "$300,000." "How much you got to spend?" "$600."

How's that going to work out?

Point being, you instead need to shrink the size of your target market to whatever resources you're willing and able to commit to allow you to have big impact. And here's the secret to that: if you want impact and you want response, then you must have repetition. They are inextricably linked. But you can't afford to do what Madison Avenue wants you to do—spend huge dollars on TV ads that play 24/7—and maybe someday respond. That's not the answer.

The answer is <u>a series of communications</u>—they could be letters, they could be emails, they could be postcards, they could be a blend—that take place over a short period of time, each one re-iterating your offer and call to action.

There's magic in the multistep structure. I'd like to claim credit for its invention, but the truth of the matter is I modeled it nearly fifty years ago. In one year, I managed to have two cars repossessed and I went personally and corporately bankrupt. I got it all over in one year.

During that year, I became intimately familiar with the collection industry and I had a lot of time on my hands. I noticed a pattern, which I'll describe to you. It's first notice, second notice, third notice. They're typically fifteen days apart, although you don't have to adhere to that timing. Each one clearly refers to the previous one they sent you. We call that linkage. There's no mystery in that they're writing to you frequently. They get a little tougher as they go along. And the last one generally has copies of everything else they sent previously, rubber-stamped "Final Notice."

I said to myself, "If that will get money from people who haven't got any, offering them nothing, I wonder what would happen if we tried it on people who do have some money and offered them something of value."

This has turned out to be one of my most reliable *Magnetic Marketing* structures, which is why it has become the staple of the Magnetic Conversion system.

ADDING MORE CREDIBILITY WITH CONTENT

A simple three-step sequence works great for many products and markets. But there are times when you need to extend the sales timeline to increase your authority and credibility. In cases like these, you probably want to consider bolstering your positioning by following up on the initial Lead Generation Magnet with additional, related content.

This strategy is done quite often when launching a brand-new product or service. The initial Lead Generation Magnet might be a video training, which is then followed up by a series of additional videos on that same topic. But you don't have to limit yourself to videos, you can follow up with any number of things, such as emails, reports, online assessments, even books.

When doing this kind of extended campaign, it's typical to hold off on asking for the sale up until the very end. Up to that point, you continue to provide valuable insights and each new piece of content ends with a "stay tuned for coming attractions" message.

The final piece of content is where you would make your real call to action—laying out all the critical elements of your offer, features, benefits, pricing, guarantee, etc.

BLOWING THEM AWAY WITH "SHOCK AND AWE"

A related idea is to bundle a bunch of perceived "high value" content items into a single package and then deliver them all at once in what's been called a "Shock and Awe" package.

The name is derived from the 1992 Gulf War, when US forces overwhelmed Saddam Hussein's military with overwhelming force. The objective with your Marketing "Shock and Awe" is likewise to overwhelm the prospect with overwhelming evidence that you are indeed head-and-shoulders above any other competitor.

Your Shock and Awe package could include:

→ Consumer Report Guide(s): Reports written by you to position you as the expert that you are.

→ CD/DVD's: Audio and/or video of interviews, guest appearances, podcasts, presentations, case studies, testimonials, etc. (anything showcasing authority and expertise).

→ Printed Special Report(s): Reports that are relevant to your message and/or the prospects challenges.

→ Newsletters: Back copies of your monthly newsletter.

→ Articles or press releases: Anything you have written or has been written about you.

→ Self-Assessment and Score Analysis Tool.

→ Testimonials: Anything and everything anyone as ever said about you, showing overwhelming proof that you are the only choice they should be going with.

→ Lead Generation Book (authored by you).

And don't limit your thinking to just serious "information"—you can include cookies, candy, toys, t-shirts, and so on. One previous client in the electronics industry, sent as a step in his conversion funnel, a briefcase with a video player built in, as well as a fresh King Cake from New Orleans. A cover letter inside recommended that the prospect watch the video (which offered the service quite nicely) while enjoying a delicious piece of cake.

Now THAT made an impact. That is how you show up like nobody else.

You'll definitely want to include at least some item with your **Call To Action**, which could lead to either a direct sale or to an in-person meeting.

SELLING A CONSULTATION VERSUS A DIRECT SALE OFFER

Most of what we've discussed so far in the Conversion System is based on the idea of using all these components to lead up to a direct sale for your product or service. The power of building this out into a sequential step-by-step process, with the Lead Generation Magnet at the very beginning leading to one after the other, is that it creates a foundation for the prospect saying "YES" through an ongoing series of micro-agreements.

→ Prospect says YES to the Lead Generation Magnet.

→ Then says YES to opening a follow up email and watching an online video.

→ Then says YES to taking an assessment sent in the mail.

→ Then says YES to reading a book sent to his home.

→ And so on and so on.

All these YES agreements build on one another, leading the prospect to feel more and more in agreement with what you have to say and offer. So when the final call to action appears, they have established the habit of saying YES to what you put before them. Of course, this doesn't guarantee the sale, but it absolutely makes it much more likely. People want to believe they behave with consistency. If you can get them to consistently say YES, you have started the ball rolling in the right direction.

However, in many industries, the actual sale can't be closed without first "selling" the prospect on agreeing to attend some kind of in-person consultation or meeting.

Typical examples could include financial advisors, insurance agents, realtors, cosmetic dentists, copywriters, IT consultants, and so forth.

In these kinds of scenarios, you're using components of your Conversion System to lead directly to accepting that Consultation Meeting—and this could involve the multistep campaign, shock and awe box, ongoing content, etc.

The Consultation is where you—one-on-one—work with the prospect through their specific situation and craft the appropriate solution to meet their needs. The call to action at the end would be to sign the contract, the check, and close the deal.

If the deal does NOT close, you do NOT give up.

Instead, you continue moving forward with whatever components of the Conversion System you deem necessary, which again, can include MORE content, MORE shock and awe, and MORE multistep campaigns of email/direct mail/postcards/etc.

How long should you keep this up?

As the old saying goes, "until they buy or die." Now, once someone does become a customer, client, or patient, we don't want our Magnetic Attraction to fade. For this reason, we continue with the Magnetic Retention System.

How I Increased Sales Over 30%!

The bottom line is that I did stuff. Yep, it is that simple. I implemented as many strategies as I could cram into a day of work. Not that mamby-pamby sequential implementation stuff, but massive simultaneous implementation of strategies and tactics. But before I get to that, let me tell you a bit about me.

When I started my carpet cleaning business in the summer of 2007 (The World Financial Implosion was right around the corner), my wife Gina suffered a severe medical problem. A blood vessel in her brain exploded and almost killed her. She spent 11 days in the neuro-ICU and many months recovering. My new business had become the only source of income. Which at the time was near zero!

I then slugged and struggled through the next four years, enduring significant financial problems culminating in the loss of his home and bankruptcy.

Through it all, I was still tenacious, strong willed, passionate and had the burning desire to win.

I started my F-A-S-T implementation journey at the Boot Camp in Washington, D.C., as a Gold member in January of 2012. My goal was to develop my company to a point where it was not necessary for me to literally be cleaning carpets every day as a technician.

My goal was to be off the truck by the end of the year. In order to accomplish this, I had to put in place many procedures, both operationally and in the marketing aspect of the company. I told myself I needed to jump start my business and make a strong showing this year or I am packing it in.

So I attended the Magnetic Marketing Boot Camp in D.C. WOW! What an Experience! That meeting changed everything I learned more in the 12 hours about marketing than I had in the last four years. I knew there was going to be a sales pitch at the end, but I had already made up my mind. **Whatever they were selling, I was buying.**

During that meeting I began the transformation of my business from commodity to exclusive. From that day on I continued to set, monitor, re-adjust and achieve my goals.

I had four goals that year: (1.) Increase revenue over 30 percent. (2.) Get off the truck. (3.) Increase job average 20 percent and rid myself of my blood- and cash-sucking clients. (4.) Increase time with family 15 percent. I achieved every goal that year. And every year thereafter. Magnetic Marketing gave me the tools and framework and I brought the energy, tenacity, will-power and the I-will-win-at-all-costs frame of mind.

How'd I Do It?

What did I do to achieve over 30 percent increase in sales year over year over year? Massive Implementation. There was not just one strategy or tactic, but close to 100 that were implemented in the past year.

Reprinted from the NO B.S. Marketing Letter September 2015

- All new education-based and direct response marketing system called PImP. Profit Implementation Package

- Multiple two-, three- and four-step lead generating, personalized letter campaigns

- Multistep and multimedia client reactivation: postcard, letter, email, videomail

- New service package and pricing plan designed to kill off tire-kicking cheapos

- Implemented the show-up-like-no-one-else-does plan with pre-job gifts encouraging reciprocity

- Four new consumer awareness guides and books with contributing authors

- Established multiple continuity plans for client retention and consistent cash flow

- Multiple "lumpy mail" campaigns for attracting, gaining and retaining joint venture partners

Oh, did I mention that I have four kids: 15, 12, 8, and 7 and live in a really rural area?

So if a guy who was bankrupt and nearly homeless can now make it to every soccer game and ballet recital, by outwitting and outsmarting not only the competition but his own franchisor (while living in an area of cows, chickens and rednecks) *and through direct response marketing filter them out and only attract the affluent,* **you can too**. No one has any excuse not to succeed if they get off their arse and friggin' IMPLEMENT!

Vance Morris is still the owner of his carpet cleaning business. He now also consults with other small businesses on how to implement Disney Style Service & Direct Response Marketing through his process of Systematic Magic.

CHAPTER 9

Your Magnetic Retention System

This is the part of the puzzle that no one does. The part that can quickly and easily turn one client into two, thus doubling the value of every new client. And the best part is it's the easiest system to implement in your business.

One of the most important keys to maximum customer value is in retention and repeat business. That is not something you're "entitled to" as a result of your excellent products and quality service—although that doesn't hurt in the least.

Instead, it's a result of careful, strategic marketing, which includes continuing to market to them in a systematic way, not taking them for granted and communicating again and again in a magnetically attractive manner.

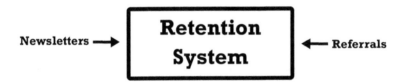

This requires frequently having and presenting a good answer to the question that is so important to us that it's become part of our vernacular. It's how we greet each other. That question is,

"What's new?"

I don't say, "Tell me everything that's the same as it was the last time I saw you three months ago." I'm not interested in that. I'm interested in *"What's new."*

If you don't have a good answer to "What's new?" they go looking for it somewhere else. A bored customer goes elsewhere. They forget about you. They don't talk about you. They don't buy from you and they are easily wooed by some competitor who comes along with something that's new and exciting.

How do you answer this question that is always on their minds? And how do you do it consistently and repetitively, so they are always intrigued by you?

The answer to this question is by frequently and continually reinventing your business inside your business, by inventing new widgets and offering those new widgets through constant communication with your past and present customers.

At least once a month, if not more often, they are hearing from you and they are getting a new widget offered to them.

That will keep customers interested and engaged, allowing you to sell to them more frequently, and having more customers refer more often.

Point is, your complete *Magnetic Marketing System* should incorporate what, in direct marketing lingo, is called "Front-end and back-end":

→ *Front-end* refers to outreach to attract and acquire new leads, new potential customers and new customers.

→ *Back-end* means developing and retaining those customers, increasing the frequency of repeat business you do with them, cross selling different products and services, putting fresh offers in front of them frequently, staying interesting to them so they stay with you and tell others about you.

How do you do that? There are two ways to include in every Magnetic Retention System:

1. CUSTOMER NEWSLETTERS

Every business should have some kind of customer newsletter that—at a minimum—hits their doorstep once a month. Preferably it would be a real, printed newsletter.

Why?

First off, it has a higher perceived value—a physical newsletter looks like it has more value than an email. Secondly, it's more likely to get consumed. An email—maybe it'll get opened, maybe not. But if you get something in the mail that you have to open up and look at, and it's at least minimally fun and interesting, then it's far more likely to get read and possibly even retained.

And that brings up the third reason a real life, honest to gosh print newsletter has value—if they keep it around, it lingers as an ongoing reminder of your existence. You're no longer a memory of some service once rendered, a product once acquired. You're there on the file cabinet letting me know that you cared enough to take the effort to send me something new rather than discard all memory of me to the dustbin of history.

Your monthly client newsletter should include:

➔ Content that re-affirms your uniqueness (remember that USP?) and authority in your business area of expertise. But keep this minimal, as little as absolutely necessary. (For heaven's sake, do NOT make your entire newsletter about your industry. Nobody wants to hear about "the latest oil filter interface to the internet of things" from their local

Qwik Lube oil change place.) Instead, you want to continue the conversation that you know they are having in their heads—continue to talk about problems you know that they have. For instance, I know that business owners who are looking to solve marketing problems are intrigued by time management strategies, ways to outsource successfully, and are looking for reassurance that they are not strange and different for their beliefs about money and capitalism. All of those have very little to do with marketing solutions, but everything to do with the people that I am talking to.

→ Content that's fun for the sake of being fun—puzzles, brainteasers, jokes, recipes, cartoons, funny "memes," light hearted fodder that offers some entertainment value—you want your customers to look forward to this every month. Puzzles and brainteaser are also what we call enticement devices. Meaning that your newsletter will have staying power while they are engaged with it.

→ In line with "what's new?" some kind of call to action for your latest widget. You are in business after all and you want to constantly remind customers that you offer valuable goods and services that will make their lives better. This is a great place to offer your newest consumer report or special report on a newsworthy topic that is plaguing them.

→ And finally, personality. When you create a bond with your customers, they are less likely to choose another provider over you, because you have become a friend. Your newsletter allows you to continue your relationships. By telling stories and sharing what is happening in your life, you let your customers bond with you.

And one the best reasons for doing all you can to retain customers, clients, or patients is to get them to refer you to their friends, family, and colleagues.

2. REFERRALS / WORD-OF-MOUTH

Word-of-mouth marketing is the most powerful and beneficial kind of advertising or marketing that you could ever have for a business for the very simple reason of what others say about you is ten times more believable than what you say about yourself.

Way back when Anaheim, California was still a swamp, Walt Disney wrote a marketing principle that was taught to everybody involved with Disney and it is a wonderful principle. It says:

"The way to be very successful in marketing is to do what you do so well that people can't resist telling others about you."

So one of the things you have to be continually asking yourself about your own business is:

How can we do what it is that we do here so well that people can't resist telling others about us?

For example, when a patient comes in the door, do you teach your staff not to sit behind the desk and kind of look up at them and grunt and hand them paperwork to fill out?

Instead, your staff should stand up, come out from around the counter, shake the patient's hand, and say: "Hi, Mr. Patient, welcome to X, Y, Z, clinic," or "Hi, Mr. Patient, good to see you today. How are you feeling?"

Then walk that patient through a greeting process unlike any other doctor's office he's ever gone to—in fact, it's unlike how he's treated anywhere else he goes to.

And a lot of those little things added together now result in what we call the wow experience. This person leaves your office and thinks to himself:

"Wow, I've got to tell somebody. This is the most interesting, amazing, best thing that's happened to me all day!"

(This relates to the "show up like no one else" principle, only it's embraced throughout your entire business, not just during conversion.)

And when you can create that for your customers, you know when they leave your place of business they're thinking: "Gee, I was feeling kind of down when I came in here, but this is the best thing that's happened to me all day. This is just wonderful."

And they run into their next door neighbor when they're now at home and they're going to tell them about you.

If you do that, they're going to spread the word without you even having to ask, and that has immense power.

When we earn this level of enthusiasm from our customers—by blowing them away with service, quality, the whole shebang, way beyond what they ever expected—we do indeed earn the right to ask. And it's amazing to me how many business people just never, in any way, shape or form, ask their customers, clients, or patients for referrals.

I grew up in direct sales, selling in the home, face-to-face with moms and dads. I was taught and beat over the head with a very simple mechanism: as soon as you make a sale, you put a card or a form and a pen in front of your customer and you said something to the effect of:

"You know, most of my customers come to me as referrals from satisfied customers like you. And I'll bet you know five or six people probably who live right here in the neighborhood who would love to have whatever it was that I was selling just like you got. And I would be eternally grateful if you would let me use your name when I gave them a call to set up an appointment. And if you would take time right now to get your Christmas card book out or you know your personal phone book and just give me those five names and addresses, I'd really appreciate it."

And nine times out of ten, I'd walk out of that house maybe not with five, but with three or four good solid names, addresses and telephone numbers and most of them would turn into appointments and some of them would turn into sales.

Now, I learned that discipline when I was a pup and I am always amazed at how many salespeople don't use it and how many business owners don't use it. A print shop owner should be asking for referrals. A dress shop owner should be asking for referrals. A hair salon/stylist should be asking for referrals.

When do you ask for referrals? Right after you've done something praiseworthy for your customer. Like when somebody comes in to pick up their job at the print shop and says:

"Boy, this is great," or "I really appreciate you bailing me out and getting this done overnight!"

That's the time for you to say something like: "Hey, you know, we're trying to grow the business here, we're taking on some new equipment and you know we really depend on clients like you for referrals. I wonder if you would just take a few of your business cards and jot down on the back of each one the name and the phone numbers of a few people that I can call and talk to."

And when you ask, you get.

Here's perfect proof of this. One of the most challenging groups I've found to convince to do referrals are chiropractors. For some reason, they seemed to have a hang up about this. Even so, we devised a plan.

They offered a back care class in their clinic that all the patients come to in a group and then they teach them about their back and how to take care of themselves. We came up with a very simple mechanism where at the end of the class the doctor essentially says:

"Oh, by the way, many of you got here as a result of being referred by somebody who cared enough about you to refer you, and that's how we get most of our new patients. We would really appreciate it if you would refer others, too. And for that reason, I am passing out these forms."

They passed out these little forms which have places for ten names, addresses and telephone numbers. And they asked them to fill them out and they're going to send them some introductory information about chiropractic.

Now, they did that very fast and it's a very soft request. It is very painless. It's done at the end of the class, so if somebody doesn't want to do it, it is easy for them to just leave the form on their chair and sneak out of the office.

Guess what happens? Seven out of ten patients fill out the form, turn in the form with somewhere between three and ten names and addresses and telephone numbers. Costs nothing to get those names, addresses and telephone numbers.

Of course, then those names, addresses and telephone numbers get plugged into the three-step campaign system and one-third of them become new patients.

All from the power of simply asking for referrals.

Margaret Good

Meet the Queen of Sales!

...and discover how Magnetic Marketing strategies helped take Margaret Good to the No. 1 rank in sales out of 37,000

In 1989, CPA Margaret Good was downsized out of her accounting job.

This inspired her to open WomenIn-BusinessMinistries.com, which has grown to empower women to reach their fullest potential, educating them about money and strategic planning.

With an eye for opportunities, Margaret capitalizes on additional businesses, too. A dog kennel, fueled by the love of dogs, operates at maximum capacity. And a Mary Kay Cosmetics business, started for the sole purpose of helping a client, turned into a major income source for her family, which works on the business together. That collaboration began when Margaret, already a Mary Kay personal use consultant, recommended her 18-year-old daughter Stephanie sign up to become a Mary Kay consultant as a summer job when she came home from college in 2014.

Since joining the Magnetic Marketing community in 2012 and implementing Magnetic Marketing, Margaret tripled her income, increased customer loyalty, wrote a book, Abundant Living (coming out in 2018) and has experience tremendous success with Mary Kay. Margaret was crowned the prestigious "Queen of Sales" a year ago, the No. 1 Mary Kay sales consultant in Canada out of 37,000 competitors. Stephanie earned her first Mary Kay career car at age 20 and became a director shortly after her 21st birthday.

Margaret says, "Since we've been listening to Dan... Stephanie now owns her own horse who's having its second foal... she is going into her fifth year of post-secondary debt-free because the business has paid for all her tuition, and she goes to a private university with no government funding."

The Fortune Is In
The Follow-Up

The biggest challenge the Goods overcame with the help of Magnetic Marketing is customer loyalty.

"It's so easy to go in and get a mascara at the Shopper's Drug Mart located at every corner instead of calling us," laments Margaret. "What really clicked with me was when Dan said it's 7 – 12 times before a customer may accept your offer." Margaret collects all the information she can – address, email, phone number – so she can follow up with different mediums at different times.

The Goods send clients a catalog quarterly, a monthly newsletter, postcards to announce open houses, and they carry samples to give out everywhere they go. They also send cards for birthdays, anniversaries, Thanksgiving, Christmas, and to say thank you. They follow up after sending mail with

Reprinted from the NO B.S. Marketing Letter February 2018

emails, phone calls and text messages, depending on the client's preferences. She says, "I'm a big emailer... but Stephanie's age group, they're more into texting."

Newsletters entertain and subtly sell by letting customers know where the Goods will be demoing product. "It gives people more freedom to come see and has made a big difference," says Margaret. Follow-up messages often simply ask if they received their newsletter.

Margaret says it's all about making the customer feel important. "People love getting mail or a card saying, 'I appreciate your business.' Those things go a long way."

Create A Monthly Club

Inspired by the Magnetic Marketing membership levels, Margaret created a monthly club. Clients join the Bronze ($20/month), Silver ($40/month), Gold ($60/month) or Platinum Club ($100/month) to receive a different package each month, themed according to what's happening. "Valentine's Day, we would focus on the lips. You might get a lip gloss and little baggie with a nice card, or for Platinum, you get chocolates and a rose," Margaret explains.

When Stuck, Get Advice

To promote the club, letters modeled after the "Famous Giorgio Letters" from the Magnetic Marketing system and tool kit are sent. Addressing the letter to men, it came from Stephanie initially, including her picture like the original Giorgio letters. The headline read, "Be your woman's hero. Sign up for this monthly program."

The first run received negative feedback. "My daughter said, 'Mom, we have to stop sending those letters out. Wives are calling asking me why I'm hitting on their husbands,'" recalls Margaret.

Margaret turned to the Magnetic Marketing community asking, "What's wrong with this? I'm following this to a T." Magnetic Marketing coached her this way: Giorgio was not a very good-looking Italian man. Your daughter is very beautiful. It was apparent that changing the signature might help.

Margaret reformatted the letter so it was now coming from her husband instead. Leveraging their 35 years of marriage, the new letter says, "If you really want to be her hero, this is a small thing you can do every month to surprise her." This time it worked.

"Keep trying different things and asking for advice, making sure you have really good mentors or a Mastermind group that you belong to," advises Margaret.

Go After Big-Money Clients

Following Dan's advice to devote more time going after people who have more money to spend in volume, Margaret began targeting cruise ship franchises by sending them a shock-and-awe package. "I put in a tin of homemade cookies, our sunscreen products, along with our foot-energizing cream and dropped it off to franchise owners," she says. Stressing the importance of showing up differently, Margaret recommended the owners sign up for her member club, using the products as thank you gifts to their customers after they book a cruise. Twenty percent of the Goods' business now comes from these clients.

Reprinted from the No B.S. Marketing Letter February 2018

CHAPTER 10

Applying The Magnetic Marketing Systems

I want to share with you a story that illustrates how a very common business owner could take everything we have discussed so far and put it into their own *Magnetic Marketing System.* It's really important that you go through it carefully. Here's why:

→ First of all, it takes everything we talked about so far and a few things we didn't, and stitches them together in chronological application order, so you see how they work.

→ Secondly, it does it in a real-life business. This is a true-life example.

→ Third, it does it in a business where most of you would never expect to find good marketing, thereby demonstrating if this guy can do it, you can do it too.

→ Fourth, it gives you a complete marketing strategy, a step-by-step system, that you can use exactly as it is described to you in this story and see results in your bank account in twenty-one days or less.

→ And there's a bonus. It gives you a new market, a farm, a group of prospects perfect

for you, which you already have access to but are not currently harvesting.

For it to do all of those things, every little nuance is important, you will want to pay close attention.

One day, in the mail, I get an envelope. The envelope is addressed to me, Mr. Dan Kennedy. It has a real live stamp on it. And in the return address corner is the name of someone I know, a colleague in business who also lived in my hometown.

> The takeaway for you is the envelope is from someone whose name I recognize. It's addressed to me. And it's got a real postage stamp on it. Not "bulk rate"—a stamp. What I've just described to you is one almost certain way to get an envelope opened. It's not the only way. Sometimes it's not the best way in a given situation, but it is a very good way.

So I open it. The letter headline says, "I suppose you're wondering why I'm writing to you about a plumber." I say to myself, "Yup, what's is this all about?"

> Second takeaway. If you want to make your marketing work, write down, "Got to get them to open it, got to get them to read it." And you've got about ten seconds from flap to trash to compel readership. Curiosity is one way to do it. Not necessarily the best, but it's the way that was used here. (By the way, it's exactly the same with email. You need have a great subject line if you want people to open and read your emails.)

The letter goes on to tell a story about how my colleague was having a party at his home on a Friday evening to which I had not been invited, and at about nine o'clock at night, a pipe in the den under the bar began to spew water everywhere.

A horrible mess.

He had to find a plumber who would come out on a Friday night at nine. Made calls out of the phone book, finally found this guy, Al the plumber, who rushed out, gooped this, tightened that, didn't have to sell him any parts. He had the whole mess cleaned up in under twenty minutes and only charged him a small amount of money.

And in order to say thank you to this plumber for this extraordinary service he decided to send this letter to all of us, his colleagues who live in town, and let us all know that if we ever need a plumber, Al's the guy we've got to call.

> There's more you have to know about the Al story. But a major money-making thing just happened. It's called a *champion circle of influence*. Everybody has a circle of influence in which you could do business if you were properly introduced, but you haven't been.

The plumber goes back to the customer and says, "You know, when I was here the other night, you were very grateful and I appreciate that. What you probably don't know is we get very little of our new business the way we got you, from advertising. We get most of our new customers through people like you, because you probably belong to something. You belong to Rotary?" "No."

"Country Club?" "No."

"Homeowners association?" "No."

"Well, everybody belongs to something."

The guy confesses. He says, "Well, there is this speakers' association I belong to."

"Great! How many of those are there in Phoenix?" "Three hundred." The plumber says, "Terrific. Here's what I'd like to do." Here's the second thing. The plumber says, "I wrote up what you said to me as I left, now as a letter from you to those three hundred people. We can change anything you want to change. But then I want to take it and I want to put it on your stationery. Again, not mine, yours. I want to put it in your envelopes. Not mine, yours. And I want to send it to those three hundred people who know you by name but do not yet know me. I pay for everything. May I do that?"

> That's called an endorsed mailing to a champion circle of influence. It's the only piece of mail on the planet that will 100 percent get opened and 100 percent get read.

So I got the envelope, opened the envelope, and read the whole letter.

And when I got all done with it, I didn't call Al the plumber.

Why didn't I call Al the plumber? Right, because I didn't need a plumber, sure. So all that's wasted, isn't it?

Wrong.

If he stops there, it's a giant epic waste.

Think of what has to happen now for it to turn into business for the plumber. I got the letter and read it. Al sounds like a pretty good guy. But I don't need a plumber.

But for this to work for Al, I'd have to make eighteen copies of this letter, then get eighteen zip-lock sandwich bags and eighteen pieces of duct tape, because he's got eighteen pipes. I'd have to put a letter in each bag, then I'd have to go around and stick one to every pipe so someday when I DO need a plumber, I can find this guy.

This is no way to get a flood of business.

That's why, about ten days later, I get what I would call letter number one from Al the plumber.

"Hi, I'm Al the plumber. You remember me? I'm the guy your friend wrote to you about, who had the party you weren't invited to, who had the leak I rushed out and took care of. Now the reason I'm writing you now is we have this very important free thing we do only for people referred to us for our VIP customers. That free thing is a free home plumbing problem-prevention audit. And the reason why it's so important for you to have a free home plumbing prevention audit is every home ten years old or older has at least one hundred horrible plumbing problems that could occur at a moment's notice. And we come out and make sure none of those things are about to happen to you, for free."

> Notice what Al's just done—he's using his "Free Home Plumbing Problem-Prevention Audit" as a Lead Generation Magnet to get me to raise my hand and invite him to provide further information. Yes, it's a consultation, but because he's already established credibility through the endorsed mailing from my buddy, the threshold barrier's been lowered enough to go with this as a first step. Of course, Al could've offered instead a more standard LGM like a report, "100 Horrible Plumbing Disasters Just Waiting to Destroy Your Home and How to Prevent Them—Guaranteed!" in his system. Again, in this situation the audit works just fine.

I still don't call Al the plumber.

Now I'm hearing drips in the night I wasn't hearing before, but I still don't call Al.

That's why ten days later, Al the plumber, sends me a second notice.

"Hi, I'm Al the plumber. You remember me? I'm the guy your friend wrote to you about, had the party you weren't invited to, had the leak. I wrote to you about our free home plumbing problem-prevention audit. I haven't heard from you and I'm very concerned. If you'll take a look at the enclosed article reprint, you'll see why."

And I take this article reprint out of the envelope. It's from a small community newspaper. Everybody knows everybody. They only publish once a week. Here's a front-page story about this couple, elderly couple. They went away just for the weekend to visit the grandkids, a little drip under the sink when they left. They put a little Tupperware bowl under there to catch it.

They come back on Monday. And in the article, there's a photograph of the house in five parts floating in a pond. There's another photograph of the family dog clinging to a piece of wood, waiting to be rescued.

I go back to the letter and it says,

"As you can see, even small plumbing problems can become big plumbing problems at a moment's notice."

I still don't call Al the plumber.

But now I'm going through the basement looking at pipes and thinking, "They look okay to me."

Ten days later, Al the plumber sends the his third "final notice" letter:

"Dan, we've twice offered you our free home plumbing problem-prevention audit. We haven't heard from you, but we sure have heard from a whole lot of other smart folks. That's why if you want the free home plumbing problem-prevention audit, it's very important you call within the next seventy-two hours. Otherwise, we may have to put you

on a waiting list of up to one hundred days. And enclosed is a list of some
of the horrible plumbing problems that may occur during...”

I call Al the plumber.

Now, I'm going to tell you the rest of the Al story in a second, but first let's do some quick analysis. Al the plumber did everything we've talked about brilliantly. Let's analyze his marketing campaign.

Al the plumber, our marketing genius, goes and he gets himself a small, carefully-selected, manageable target market. His is his *champions circle of influence*, one of the most productive farms you'll ever own.

The first seed he plants in his farm is the endorsed mailing, the only piece of mail that 100 percent gets delivered, 100 percent gets opened, 100 percent gets read.

He then kicks off his campaign with a sequence of communications.

He creates a Lead Generation Magnet, which is the offer of a free in-home plumbing audit.

He continues to pound this offer, referencing prior mailings, adding urgency with a final notice.

He did everything we talked about brilliantly.

And if a plumber can do it, you can do it too.

Now let's talk about showing up like no one else.

Al arrives at my home, virtually no resemblance to what I expect when I think "plumber." He's not wearing work-clothes, he's not carrying a tool box.

Al the plumber is in a three-piece suit, freshly pressed white shirt, quality tie, and shined shoes. He's carrying a brown calf-skin attaché case.

The only resemblance between this business executive and a plumber is on the breast pocket of his suit coat, there's a cloth patch sewn on that says, "Al."

He comes into the house, he opens up his attaché case, takes out a matching clipboard.

"Mr. Kennedy, as you can see, this is the form I'm going to use to check the one hundred possible plumbing problems. It takes me about twenty minutes to do that. While I do that, do you have a DVD player? You need to watch this DVD."

I watch the DVD which talks about one of the greatest health care crises in America today.

Seems an alarming number of us seasoned citizens are falling and slipping in our bathtubs. Serious injuries, breaking hips. It turns out they've got this invisible glop that replaces bathmats forever, one-time application. Nothing to clean, and you'll never slip and fall. A lifetime warranty.

The video clicks off in nineteen minutes.

And as it does, Al is standing there.

Obviously, Al has done this before.

"Mr. Kennedy, I have very good news for you. You do not have ninety-six of the most common household plumbing problems. The ones you do have are very trivial. I have everything with me to take care of them today. I just need to go out and get some work clothes and get some tools. While I do that, did you watch the DVD?"

Yep, I watched it.

"I noticed you have five baths. You have one in the master suite, then you have these other four. While I'm here today, shall we just protect the

one in the master suite or shall we protect all of them?"

$389 later, Al the plumber gets in his new Lexus and drives away.

I was intrigued so I called him a few days later, "Look, I didn't want to bother you when you were out at the house working. I know that's rude. But I teach Magnetic Marketing Systems and you used one of them brilliantly. I wonder if you'd mind sharing the numbers?"

Al says, "Not at all, I'll just have to put you on hold and get the project file."

I'm now on hold, listening to a recorded commercial for his brother's pool cleaning service. When that's over, he's back.

"What would you like to know?"

"How many homes did you mail to?"

"About three hundred."

"How many of those home problem-prevention audit things have you done so far?"

"Seventy-two."

Do the math, if you wish. Assume no one but me gave him money immediately. A poor assumption on your part, but make it if you wish.

For the price of three hundred letters times three, he's been in seventy-two homes where he's put on a show and a half.

When they need a plumber, who are they going to call?

To make sure, at every place there's a pipe, there's a sticker.

Of course Al's newsletter "Plumber's Helper" arrives within the week.

Again... who are they going to call?

You get the picture.

THAT is how you work the *Magnetic Marketing System*, soup to nuts. And if a business like a plumber could do it, it's a pretty sure bet your business can do so as well.

Member Spotlight:

Rafal Dyrda

Ultimate Independence

How Rafal Dyrda Built His Dream Lifestyle Of Working Just Four Hours A Month

It started when Rafal Dyrda read The 4-Hour Workweek by Tim Ferriss. "Once I read that book, my goal was to build that type of business where I worked four hours a week and enjoyed life."

Exacerbated by losing important people in his life, it wasn't just financial freedom Rafal wanted, it was more time to do the things he and his wife, Kinga, enjoy such as hiking, biking, and snowboarding. He also wanted to move to a city surrounded by mountains, a beautiful lake and that had four seasons.

On June 15th, Rafal and Kinga moved into their dream home. Located in Kelowna, British Columbia, Canada, their home is within a one-hour drive to multiple ski resorts.

"My parents immigrated from Poland back in the 1980s and it took them a long time to get back on their feet. Because I saw how they struggled when I was a kid ... I was really driven to create a life for myself where I wasn't dependent on anybody."

Not only did Rafal reach his goal of working just four hours per week, he surpassed it. "I built my business where I actually only have to work about four hours a month," Rafal said.

Living By Design

Everything from how Rafal hires employees, to how he funds his company, is done deliberately, although Rafal's company, GeniePad.com, was born out of frustration. Genie Pad helps condominiums and homeowner associations improve communication, collaboration and access to information so that work is completed on time, homeowners are happy, and less time is spent in board meetings.

In 2003, Rafal Dydra bought his first condo. At the time he thought, "stress-free living. Everything is taken care of for you. This is going to be great."

Until he and Kinga came back from vacation to find their storage room flooded with no idea who to contact. The number they were given when they moved in was out of service. They didn't know who the management company was or who was on the board. By a total fluke, Rafal ran into the board president and was able to get the issue resolved. Another issue popped up, which took the board six months to complete. After voicing his opinions at his condo's first annual general meeting, he was nominated to sit on the board.

"As soon as I joined the board, I understood why things were happening the way they were," Rafal said. "There were no systems in place. There was no transparency. No tracking of any

Reprinted from the NO B.S. Marketing Letter July 2018

work requests or anything like that."

When the first board meeting took three hours, Rafal realized he couldn't dedicate the time required to volunteer and help manage his 220 unit condominium. A software consultant, he built a portal to help manage things and facilitate communication. When the property manager saw what Rafal created, she said, "I need this for my other properties. Can I have a copy?"

"It wasn't really meant to be a product," Rafal said, "but I said, you know what, I'll do it. At the time it was replicated to eight other properties. In 2010, I launched this to the public and people started signing up."

As the product gained traction, he fired his consulting clients and focused on Genie Pad 100%.

Today Rafal has clients across Canada and the U.S. and employs a small team of under 10 employees which he says are fantastic. "I don't want to work with just anybody," Rafal said. "I work with smart, committed, driven people … that want something more out of life than just to make an income … and like to have this type of lifestyle."

Choose To Be Different

Most software start-up companies go after funding and venture capital. Not Rafal. "Because I wanted to build more of a lifestyle business to have the time freedom, I decided to fund the company by myself," Rafal reflected. "Back then I didn't have a lot of capital to invest in a huge team, so I had to look at solutions of how I could automate as much of the process as possible … and I bumped into Infusionsoft."

Watching video presentations from a previous Infusionsoft conference, he heard Darcy Juarez speak. "She was presenting on direct response marketing," Rafal recalled. "I'm thinking, this lady is really smart, and she's talking about all these things that I'm trying to do." Rafal admits, at the time, he didn't know what direct response marketing was and that it was a radically different approach than what he'd heard from the online crowd he was following.

At the end of Darcy's presentation, she recommended Dan Kennedy's book, No B.S. Direct Marketing: The Ultimate No Holds Barred Kick Butt Take No Prisoners Direct Marketing for Non-Direct Marketing Businesses, which Rafal purchased.

"I read the book in one day," Rafal said. "I didn't have a marketing background or education in sales or anything like that. I was a software developer, turned consultant. It really pulled me in because it actually made sense."

Rafal requested the free offer at the end of the book, purchasing Magnetic Marketing next. Fast Implementation Boot Camp followed. "Dave Dee made an offer for the Ultimate Marketing Machine and I bolted out of my chair," Rafal recalled.

"Right now, I spend more money on my education per year than my entire college education cost."

Rafal designates every single Friday as an education day, focusing on learning something new and then implementing that in his business. He didn't start that way though. "Initially I bought these Magnetic Marketing products that were shrink-wrapped and I didn't open them," Rafal confessed, "Once I dedicated Fridays as my education day and started implementing the marketing principles Magnetic Marketing gives on a silver platter, that is when things started changing."

He implemented the Ultimate Marketing Machine program, including writing a book, The Condo Board Survival Guide, and sending out direct mail, which he'd never done before. Attending SuperConference and Info-Summit were next. And he joined Peak Performers four years ago to hold himself accountable.

"Once I implemented that whole system," Rafal said, "I started seeing huge, huge benefits and growth."

His revenue increased 25% the first year. "Since then, just by implementing the Magnetic Marketing strategies alone, my revenue increases between 30 and 40 percent every year."

Rafal's Secret To Implementation

"If I read something and find value and believe that it's going to work, I have to implement right away," Rafal said. "Sometimes I would start on a Friday and I would work through the weekends just to get it done. The key here is ... you have to act on it right away. Don't wait too long. That's the mistake I originally made and why I joined Peak Performers."

"You have to build a system, not just a campaign."

"What Magnetic Marketing really helped me with is the entire marketing system," Rafal said. "It's not just generating leads or converting them .. it's the whole system. Most people focus on the little bits and pieces. You have to dig deep and go further." Rafal said you have to look at what's happening

before they become a customer, during and after. Investing in the right tools, technology, and CRM has helped him create a system that does most of the work automatically for him which has increased his profits and given him time freedom.

Build Loyal Customers

Understanding his audience, their pain points, struggles and language has been a huge key to his success. "I realized my clients needed more training and education and that it takes them a bit longer to make a decision."

Analyzing results helps him understand. For example, people watched between 70 to 75 percent of his video before they converted. This revelation made him realize he needed to start building a relationship with his clients. "As Dan says, you have to become a welcome guest and not a pest," Rafal said. "I merged marketing and sales with education and that's when I really started building trust with my clients."

His approach not only wins over clients, it creates loyal ones. "I have clients that signed up with me in 2010 and are still clients today," Rafal shared, "And because I work on a recurring revenue model, they pay me a monthly fee. That's why the company goes nicely because we retain our clients for a very, very long time."

Include Video To Build Authority

"People come up to me and say, 'it's great to finally meet you,'" Rafal shared. "I've never met this person in my life, but they have a relationship with me because they were watching my videos and reading my stuff."

Reprinted from the NO B.S. Marketing Letter July 2018

In addition to his book (http://condoboardbook.com), Rafal writes blog posts and creates videos, including an interview series (http://condowebshow.com). "You have to be an authority, celebrity, and expert in your industry," Rafal said, "And I feel video is one of the best media sources right now."

"It's amazing people don't tap into Facebook Live, Instagram Live and YouTube much because right now it's fresh and still growing," Rafal continued. "So, it's best to be one of the first people in your industry that does it."

"Anybody in any industry can do this," Rafal encouraged, "If you're a lawyer, if you're a physical therapist if you do carpet cleaning ... if you're good at what you do, you'll be able to provide some tips to your clients and provide them some value."

Do you dream of a 4-hour work week? Follow Rafal's lead: Automate as much as possible. Make yourself the authority. And implement. One last piece of advice, "You're not going to get all the answers at a conference or by listening to a podcast," Rafal said. "You have to dig deeper, go further. You have to invest in yourself, you have to commit the time." When you do, you'll be rewarded.

CHAPTER 11

What To Do Now

Now It's Up to You

"When you come to a fork in the road, take it."

— Yogi Berra

There are three steps to positive change:

1. Awareness

2. Decision

3. Action

With this book, I have provided <u>Awareness</u>. There is a better, more productive, more differentiated approach to growing a business by applied attraction rather than by pursuit; by focused, targeted marketing rather than mud-against-wall and hope; and by an organized system rather than random and erratic acts.

Now you face a <u>Decision</u> that is entirely yours to make. The legendary attorney Gerry Spence almost always closed his ending speech to juries by telling an old, old parable about the wise man and the smart-aleck boy. The wise elder made himself available every Saturday for the villagers to line up and ask for his advice. The boy resented his authority, and developed a plan to humiliate "Mr. Know

It All." The boy captured a small bird and concealed it in his hands, and stood before the wise man and asked if the bird in his hands was alive? Or was it dead? If the wise man said "Alive," the boy intended to quickly crush it to death and let it fall to the ground. If the wise man said "Dead," the boy would open his hands and let it fly free. But the wise man proved truly wise with his answer: "Son, that bird is in *your* hands."

Whether you end with having read this book, nodded in places, wished you could remake your business to be "magnetic" but default to continuing to conduct business just as you do now and as your competitors do—*or* you can take the next steps to a road less traveled with great potential—is entirely in *your* hands. Frankly, the person who reads but does act is no better off than the illiterate dunce who cannot read. The person who endlessly procrastinates and excuses himself from decisive action is no better than the somnambulant sloth.

The road to ruin is paved with good intentions. And, as an old saying goes, "*if wishes were horses, every man afoot would ride.*" Creative, constructive Action is what actually brings about positive change.

There is good news about Action. Business today is complicated. It is easy to feel overwhelmed. Are you too busy just making a living to make any real money? Or a better life? That is understandable but should be unacceptable. So, that is where the organization built around The Magnetic Marketing System® can step in, step up, and work right alongside you in implementing a series of dramatic breakthroughs. Those next steps are offered on the very next page.

You can soon own a fully functional business and profit building SYSTEM of your own… *or*… you can continue as you are.

That bird is in *your* hands.

Never Again Be An Advertising Victim, Discover The Secrets To Creating A Successful Advertising and Marketing System For Your Business, Products and Services...

Get THE System That Business Owners Just Like You Have Used To Radically Transform Their Advertising From Ineffective and Wasteful Into A Business Asset That Will Predictably and Reliably Deliver A Steady Stream Of New Customers, Clients, Patients and

Profits to the Bottom Line!

In This Master Class, You'll Discover:

- The difference between **Lead Generation** and **Brand Building**, and why lead generation almost always **TRUMPS** the latter.

- In most cases, THIS one form of advertising is only **wasting your time and money** for **minimal results.**

- THIS form of advertising will have you **seeing returns in days, weeks, or months** instead of wondering what the expense brought to you in return a year down the road.

- How YOU can be successful **without having to worry about how many people know your brand by name.**

- Learn how advertising in certain media outlets that have **nothing** to do with your business can actually make **A LOT** of sense and be **very beneficial.**

- How to **model** the marketing strategies of national companies in a way that will their success into a local level.

4 Amazing Bonus Gifts Valued at $938.97

Bonus Gift 1:
FREE Lead Generation Advertising Mastery Video Master Class
$297.00 Value

Bonus Gift 2:
The Best Of Dan Kennedy Collection
$497.97 Value

Bonus Gift 3:
Dan Kennedy's 10 Rules Of Direct Response Advertising Check List
$47.00 Value

Bonus Gift 4:
30 Day *FREE Trial* of the 'Famous' No B.S. Marketing Newsletter and Magnetic Marketing Gold Membership
$97.00 Value

ABOUT THE AUTHOR

Dan Kennedy with the Magnetic Marketing team authored this official guide to Magnetic Marketing®, in which he challenges entrepreneurs and business owners to dump the boring, conventional, common advertising and marketing that commoditizes them into "sameness" and dooms them to chasing customers and begging for their business. Why not attract them instead, and have them standing in line to do business with you?

Dan Kennedy is founder of Magnetic Marketing® | No B.S. Inner Circle and one of the most revered marketing advisors to entrepreneurs and business owners in the world. Kennedy has taught his Magnetic Marketing System to over 6 million people around the world. For nine consecutive years, Kennedy spoke on the famous *SUCCESS* Tour, earning on average $100,000 per speech, and sharing the stage with business leaders like Debbi Fields (Mrs. Fields Cookies) and Ben & Jerry; popular business speakers Zig Ziglar, Brian Tracy, Tom Hopkins and Tony Robbins; entertainment and sports celebrities Larry King, Johnny Cash, and Mary Tyler Moore; even former Presidents including Ronald Reagan and other world leaders like Gen. Colin Powell, Margaret Thatcher and Mikail Gorbachev. Kennedy has delivered over three thousand paid speeches and seminars to entrepreneurs and business owners. Kennedy has authored thirty-two books, named to the "Top 100 Business Books" list by *Inc.* Magazine, translated in a dozen languages, and often earning spots on Amazon

Bestseller Lists. Kennedy has been interviewed or featured in three hundred different business magazines, trade journals and newsletters including *Forbes, Bloomberg BusinessWeek,* and *Entrepreneur.* If you want to attract new customers and grow your business, there is no other advisor and thought-leader better suited and committed to that outcome than Dan Kennedy and Magnetic Marketing.

OTHER BOOKS BY DAN S. KENNEDY

Speak to Sell (Advantage)

Make 'Em Laugh & Take Their Money (GKIC/Morgan-James)

The Ultimate Sales Letter – 4th Edition/20th Anniversary Edition
  (Adams Media)

The Ultimate Marketing Plan – 4th Edition/20th Anniversary Edition
  (Adams Media)

Making Them Believe: 21 Lost Secrets of Dr. Brinkley Marketing with
  Chip Kessler (GKIC/Morgan-James)

My Unfinished Business/Autobiographical Essays (Advantage)

The NEW Psycho-Cybernetics with Maxwell Maltz, M.D., F.I.C.S.
  (Prentice-Hall)

In the No B.S. series, published by Entrepreneur Press

No B.S. Guide to Maximum Referrals & Customer Retention with
  Shaun Buck

No B.S. Guide to Direct-Response Social Media Marketing with Kim
  Walsh Phillips

No. B.S. Guide to Brand-Building by Direct Response

No. B.S. Guide to Trust-Based Marketing with Matt Zagula

No. B.S. Guide to Marketing to Boomers & Seniors with Chip Kessler

No. B.S. Price Strategy with Jason Marrs

No. B.S. Ruthless Management of People & Profits, 2nd Edition

No B.S. Grassroots Marketing with Jeff Slutsky

No. B.S. Business Success in the New Economy

No. B.S. Sales Success in the New Economy

No. B.S. Wealth Attraction in the New Economy

No. B.S. Time Management for Entrepreneurs, 3rd Edition

No. B.S. Guide to Powerful Presentations with Dustin Mathews